Strength and Diversity in Social Work with Groups
Think Group

"A coherent and comprehensive collection of articles that inform us about practice with a diversity of groups and ignite excitement about their breadth and potential. As you journey from one article to another, it is impossible to lay the book down. I thank the editors for their labor of love in putting together this uniquely informative collection and strongly recommend it to you."

Alex Gitterman, Zachs Professor of Social Work,
University of Connecticut, USA

How can groups effectively meet the needs of humans in areas as diverse as aid, responsibility, action, healing, learning, and acceptance? This edited volume aims to address these issues and provide ways to extend the current reach and quality of social work with groups.

Based on a selection of papers from the 24th Annual International Symposium of the Association for the Advancement of Social Work with Groups (AASWG) the chosen chapters embody the strength and diversity of the Symposium, encouraging readers to "Think Group." Chapters address the future challenges faced in social work with groups, including issues in teaching group work, holistic thinking about groups, team-building, staff development programs and university–agency collaborations to strengthen group work practice. There are chapters focusing on how mutual aid groups support trauma recovery, including one with firemen addressing the aftermath of the 9/11 disaster, as well as chapters that examine group work's place in community development, challenging social isolation, mask making as a medium for growth, and special issues in addressing concerns of children and youth.

This book will be of interest to researchers, professionals, and students in social work and human service fields.

Carol S. Cohen is Associate Professor in the School of Social Work at Adelphi University, USA.

Michael H. Phillips is Professor Emeritus in the Graduate School of Social Service at Fordham University, USA.

Meredith Hanson is Professor in the Graduate School of Social Service at Fordham University, USA.

Strength and Diversity in Social Work with Groups
Think Group

**Edited by
Carol S. Cohen,
Michael H. Phillips and
Meredith Hanson**

 Routledge
Taylor & Francis Group

NEW YORK AND LONDON

First published 2009
by Routledge
270 Madison Ave, New York, NY 10016

Simultaneously published in the UK
by Routledge
2 Park Square, Milton Park, Abingdon, Oxon OX14 4RN

Routledge is an imprint of the Taylor & Francis Group, an informa business

Typeset in Sabon by
Swales & Willis, Exeter, Devon
Printed and bound in the United States of America on acid-free paper by
Edwards Brothers, Inc.

Library of Congress Cataloging in Publication Data
    Strength and diversity in social work with groups: think group/
    Carol S. Cohen, Michael H. Phillips, Meredith Hanson, editors.
        p. cm.
    Collection of proceedings of the 2002 International Symposium of
    the AASWG.
    1. Social group work—Study and teaching—United States—
    Congresses. I. Cohen, Carol S., 1950–   II. Phillips, Michael H.
    III. Hanson, Meredith.
    HV45. T53 2008
    361.4—dc22   2007051966

ISBN 10: 0–7890–3790–4 (hbk)
ISBN 10: 0–7890–3791–2 (pbk)
ISBN 10: 0–203–88371–3 (ebk)

ISBN 13: 978–0–7890–3790–9 (hbk)
ISBN 13: 978–0–7890–3791–6 (pbk)
ISBN 13: 978–0–203–88371–6 (ebk)

Contents

Figures

About the Editors

Carol S. Cohen, DSW, is an Associate Professor at the Adelphi University School of Social Work. Her work in the areas of group work, field and classroom teaching, supervision, agency-based practice, and community development has been published and disseminated nationally and internationally. She is a current Board Member of the AASWG. Her proposal, "Global Group Work," building a network of social group work educators throughout the world, was funded by the International Association of Schools of Social Work. Before joining the academic ranks, she held leadership positions with Catholic Charities of Brooklyn and Queens, focusing on community development, youth and family services, evaluation, and training.

Michael H. Phillips, DSW, is Professor Emeritus at the Fordham University Graduate School of Social Service and remains intensely connected to practice, agencies, and organizations. He is a former Treasurer of the AASWG and has conducted influential research projects and authored publications in program evaluation, group work practice, and organizational development. Articles, chapters, and reports related to social work with groups have included work on teaching group work and groups in teaching, incorporating resiliency themes in practice, confidentiality and norms for outside contacts, and focus group research methods.

Meredith Hanson, DSW, is a Professor and Director of the Ph.D. Program in Social Work at the Fordham University Graduate School of Social Service. His teaching, practice, and scholarly interests include group work practice in addictions, evidence-based practice, homelessness, and cross-national social work practice and education. He has published several articles and book chapters in these areas, and has presented many papers at local, national and international conferences.

Contributors

Nina L. Aronoff, Ph.D., LICSW, Assistant Professor of Social Work and MSW Program Director, Wheelock College, Boston, Massachusetts.

Darlyne Bailey, Ph.D., MSW, Dean, College of Education and Human Development, University of Minnesota. Minneapolis Minnesota.

Alma Carten, DSW, MSW, Assistant Professor, New York University School of Social Work, New York.

Diane Connolly, Ph.D., MSW, Assistant Commissioner, Office of Quality Improvement of the NYC Administration for Children's Services, New York.

Mark Doel, Ph.D., MA, CQSW, Professor of Social Work, Centre for Health and Social Care Research, Sheffield Hallam University, Sheffield, England.

Christy Driscoll, LCSW-R, 2007 Graduate of New York University College of Nursing, New York.

Arielle Dylan, MSW, MA, Honours BA, Doctoral Candidate, University of Toronto, Canada.

Keith T. Fadelici, LCSW, Assistant Director, Victims Assistance Services, Westchester, New York; Adjunct instructor, Adelphi University School of Social Work; Private Practitioner, Poughkeepsie, New York.

Sheldon R. Gelman, Ph.D., Professor and Dean, Wurzweiler School of Social Work of Yeshiva University, New York.

George S. Getzel, DSW, Professor Emeritus, Hunter College School of Social Work.

Roselle Kurland, Ph.D. (Deceased), Professor, Hunter College School of Social Work, New York.

Deborah S. Langosch, Ph.D., LCSW, Clinical Coordinator, Loss and Bereavement Program, Center for Trauma Program Innovation, Jewish

Board of Family and Children's Services; Child and Adult Psychotherapist, Project Director, Kinship Care Program, New York.

Nuala Lordan, B.Soc.Sc., M.Soc.Sc. (retired) Former Course Director of the BSW, University College Cork; Member of the University's Board of Governors, Cork, Ireland.

Andrew Malekoff, MSW, Executive Director/CEO for North Shore Child and Family Guidance Center, Roslyn Heights, New York; Journal Editor, *Social Work with Groups.*

John Marchini, MSW, LCSW, Employee Assistance Program Specialist, Fire Department of New York Counseling Service Unit, New York.

Helen B. Mullin, LCSW, BCD, Psychotherapist and Substance Abuse Specialist, Federation Employment and Guidance Service, Manhattan Counseling Center; Formerly with the Jewish Board of Family and Children's Services; Adjunct Professor, New York University, New York.

Deirdre Quirke, B.Sc. (Social Work), C.Q.S.W. Director, Fieldwork Instruction Unit at Brothers of Charity, Cork, Ireland.

Robert Salmon, DSW, Professor, Hunter College School of Social Work, New York.

Evelyn F. Slaght, Ph.D., MSW, Associate Professor, School of Social Work, Illinois State University, Normal, Illinois.

Virginia Strand, DSW, Professor, Fordham University Graduate School of Social Service, New York.

Peter B. Vaughan, Ph.D., MSW, MA, Dean, Fordham University Graduate School of Social Service, New York.

Mary Wilson, B.Soc.Sc., Dip.Social Work, C.Q.S.W., Ph.D., BSW Course Director, University College Cork, Ireland.

Introduction

*Carol S. Cohen, Michael H. Phillips,
and Meredith Hanson*

XXIV AASWG Symposium

New York City was the center of social work practice with groups in the fall of 2002, when approximately 500 people joined together to look at how *"Thinking Group"* could serve as a way of addressing the strength and diversity in social work with groups: this was the 24th Annual International Symposium of the Association for the Advancement of Social Work with Groups (AASWG), held at the Brooklyn Marriott Hotel. The Symposium was an experience of thinking, living, and learning in groups. The three-day Symposium included over 170 exciting presentations, including mobilizing addresses, dynamic workshops, intriguing papers, interactive panels, exciting displays and many opportunities for networking and discussion, conducted by over 250 presenters and chairpersons.

When we began to develop the conference theme we thought about the diversity of settings in which groups could be used and, further, the many strengths that group skills bring to solving a range of problems. We wondered what idea could unify all these thoughts. Suddenly the unifying theme for the Symposium theme appeared right before our eyes—a large billboard, above Tenth Avenue in Manhattan, New York City, proclaimed *Think Different* with a giant portrait of Albert Einstein and a modestly sized (by billboard standards) Apple Computer logo in the corner. Apple's advertising campaign was designed to celebrate creativity and those who "push the human race forward" (Ono, 1997). Perhaps the same could be said for the potential of groups to geometrically expand the benefits and power of members to move ahead. Not by coincidence, Apple's campaign was launched at a time when the computer company was experiencing plunging market share and diminishing stock value, accompanied by sagging employee morale (Elliot, 1998). In a compelling parallel, we face the prospect of decreased utilization of groups in human service settings and declining numbers of social workers with group work expertise as we move forward in social work practice.

We saw these spiraling trends and transformed *Think Different* to *Think Group*. Sadly, using a group frame of reference is all too often a *different* way of thinking in social work, but one that is nonetheless exciting and empowering. As an "enterprise of mutual aid" (Schwartz, 1971) social work with groups is indeed *different* from work with individuals, as it involves member to member exchange and places the source of growth in the membership, in the geometric effects of giving and accepting help among members (Cohen, 1993).

Thus, *Think Group* became our theme and working mantra as we engaged in the planning process. Returning to our original thinking we decided that we needed to reintegrate the strength of groups. Hence we needed to include the term *strength* to signify the intense value and power of the group for its members and the potential of group methods in social work. *Diversity* was also selected to convey the wide range of members, settings, approaches, and communities in which thinking group makes a profound difference and through which groups draw much of their power (Johnson & Johnson, 2000). The chapters included in this book embody both the strength and diversity of the Symposium, and represent the intense spirit and high level of scholarship of the presentations.

Almost immediately, we connected with the construct of *thinking group,* coined by Ruth Middleman and Gail Goldberg Wood as one concept that lies at the heart of our work with groups (1990). It involves using a group lens as the frame for seeing what is going on around us and involves viewing the group as a vehicle through which individual change occurs (Sundel, Glasser, Sarri, & Vinter, 1985). While thinking group may be divergent, our clients and communities hunger for the connections promised by collective experience. As Lewis Lowy said 50 years ago, "individuals want to gain satisfactions from group participation; they want to learn and to feel that they are part of a larger whole to which they can make a personal contribution" (1955, p. 62). Making such contributions and receiving benefits in exchange is the essence of mutual aid, and a dynamic we sought to encourage in the Symposium participation experience.

The theme of *Think Group,* provided a context for us to examine how groups effectively meet compelling human needs, as sources of aid, responsibility, action, healing, learning, and acceptance. As Hirayama and Hirayama suggest, a group can be a "reservoir of power resources where individual participants can get help and receive support" (1986, p. 124). The AASWG International Symposium is such a reservoir, from which participants can dip a cup or dive right in for an immersion in group work thinking. In 1979, the first Symposium was mounted "to reestablish social group work and its value system as a major force in the development of the social work profession" (Abels & Abels, 1981). While some progress has been achieved, we are still moving towards the realization of this goal.

The success of the 24th Symposium had seemed impossible a year before, when the hotel in which the symposium was to be held was destroyed in the World Trade Center attack. Reflecting on those days, it is clear that the power of groups made it possible to move on. The AASWG Board and groups of members encouraged us and gave rousing support as we worked with our remarkable planning committee to find another venue and keep going forward. As organizers, we attempted to *think group* at every turn, and harnessed the power of planning in group settings to bring together all the elements of the symposium so that the whole became greater than the sum of its parts. Groups and organizations throughout the world invested in the Symposium, making it a memorable and affecting experience.

Participants from throughout the world came with a wide variety of interests and experiences. As noted in their evaluations, some found the symposium "reinvigorating" and found that it "got the creative juices flowing." For others, it was "awesome to meet, see and hear social work pioneers," and "connect with others who share the passion for work with groups." Many commented on the "warmth," "generosity," as well as "high quality" of presentations and discussions. It is particularly gratifying to hear participants were able to find and generate many ideas to take back to their work, and extend to impact of the symposium beyond the four days that we were together.

We were enormously gratified that agencies, organizations, and educational institutions generously signed on as co-sponsors. Among these agencies were the Jewish Board of Family and Children's Services, Children's Aid Society, Catholic Charities of Brooklyn and Queens, Big Brothers and Big Sisters of New York City, and the Henry Street Settlement. Joining with AASWG as co-sponsors were the New York City and New York State Chapter of NASW and the United Way of New York City. Our local AASWG Chapters (Red Apple and Long Island) were of enormous assistance. The Council on Social Work Education sent a reporter to cover the Symposium for their newsletter, and an article highlighting the participation of field instructors appeared in the issue following the Symposium (Fanney, 2003).

Fordham University served as Host University, and provided a wide range of in-kind and direct financial assistance, including printing, postage, student assistantships, and staff time. Adelphi University, Columbia University, Hunter College, New York University, Stony Brook University, and Yeshiva University served as co-sponsors. We worked within existing social work education networks, including field instruction, and recruited liaisons from each local school of social work. We drew over 100 student volunteers from a wide range of social work programs in the Metropolitan New York Area.

The Symposium began with eight half-day Institutes: these were Group Work with Workers Regarding Trauma, Effective Clinical Group Work Strategies and Interventions, Spirituality in Social Work Practice with Groups, Challenges in Middles of Groups, Teaching Personal and Social Development through Adventure-Based Practice, Helping Children through Mutual Aid Activity Groups When the World No Longer Feels Safe, Field Instruction of Social Work with Groups, Focus Groups and the Community-Based Organization. There were also five "outstitutes," conducted at multiple community-based sites, at exemplary agency settings in New York City, namely the Community School Program of the Children's Aid Society,

Fountain House Clubhouse Program, Lesbian, Gay, Bisexual, & Transgender Community Center, Van Cortlandt Village Naturally Occurring Retirement Community, and Village AIDS Network and Rivington House.

Our extraordinary plenary speakers and respondents set the tone, focused on the importance of groups, and gave a call to action to participants. They included William Bell, Commissioner of the NYC Administration for Children's Services, and Barbara Rittner of the University of Buffalo at the Beulah G. Rothman Memorial Lecture at the opening banquet; Darlyne Bailey, Vice President for Academic Affairs and Dean, Teachers College, Columbia University, at the Sumner Gill Memorial Lecture on Friday; Pete Moses, Executive Director of the Children's Aid Society, group members of the "Life Lines" group of the Center for Family Life, and group members of the Children's Aid Society 9/11 Support Group at the plenary luncheon on Saturday; and Robert Salmon and Roselle Kurland, Hunter College School of Social Work, at the plenary breakfast on Sunday.

As part of the symposium, the AASWG was proud to honor four people who have made extraordinary contributions to social work with groups. Pamela Cavallo, who passed away in the preceding year, was a social worker whose love of people, ability to connect with physically challenged individuals, and excitement for innovation and growth were hallmarks of her life and her career. She was always ahead of the field in her determination to identify and implement new program models, particularly use of groups with thousands of people with multiple sclerosis, their families, and the healthcare professionals who support them. Daniel Kronenfeld served as the Executive Director of the Henry Street Settlement from 1985 through 2002, following his work as the founding director of the Settlement's Urban Family Center for 13 years, the first transitional shelter for homeless families in New York City. At the shelter, Danny demonstrated his commitment to the use of group methods to help families establish solid support networks. In addition to expanding Henry Street's size, stature, and scope, Danny strengthened and expanded the Settlement's services to now reach over 100,000 people each year on the Lower East Side and in other parts of the City.

George Getzel was honored upon his retirement, for his 28 years on the faculty of the Hunter College School of Social Work. A gifted teacher and prolific scholar, George made a profound contribution to his students' professional development and to the profession's literature, modeling a commitment to advocacy and social justice and to creative group work practice. His contribution in the area of work with people suffering with HIV/AIDS was groundbreaking, demanding professional vision and courage. Marcos Leiderman, Professor Emeritus of the Rutgers University School of Social Work in New Brunswick, where he had a long and illustrious career as a director of its group work program, migrated to the United States in 1964 after having played a leadership role in the opposition to Juan Peron. Always committed to social justice, he played pivotal roles in the AASWG, serving as two terms as the Secretary/Treasurer, Chair of the Seventh Annual

Symposium in 1985, first Chair of the Chapter Development Committee, and organizer and first Chair of the New Jersey Chapter. Danny, George, and Marcos were present to receive their awards, along with friends and family of Pam and all of the honorees.

The Symposium would not have been possible without the strong support of the AASWG Board, particularly from Toby Berman-Rossi and Tim Kelly and from other former Symposium Chairs and Coordinators including those from Toronto, Akron, Denver, and NYC. As always, John and Carol Ramey made an incredible contribution behind the scenes throughout the planning process, and on site in pulling together the membership table and coordinating the syllabus exchange and sale of books published by CSWE and Haworth Press, available to members with discounts. In addition, we received in-kind contributions from New York City & Company and Health First. We were also supported by many advertisers—there were 23 pages of ads in the final program.

Members of the Symposium Planning Committee served over a three-year period—without them this event would have not been possible.

Michael Ash	Linda Hutton
Martin Birnbaum	Roselle Kurland
Angel Campos	Maxine Lynn
Lois Carey	Andrew Malekoff
Marianne Chierchio	Susan Mason
Susan Ciardiello	Joseph Moore
Andrew Cicchetti	Marilynn Myles
Letitia Coburn	Danielle Nisivoccia
Barbara Dane	Catherine Papell
George Getzel	Rosa Perez-Koenig
Urania Glassman	Roberta Rohdin
Mary Pender Greene	Robert Salmon
Andrew Hamid	Christine Theuma
Ella Harris	Sylvana Trabout
Loretta Hartley-Bangs	Michael Wagner

All provided key areas of expertise and connection. With great delight we note that when we met three weeks after the Symposium everyone was in great spirits and honored our collective work as a vehicle that brought the Symposium to life and brought us closer at the same time.

Over the next three days, there were wonderful social opportunities to *Think Group*, including a send off by Marty Markowitz, Borough President of Brooklyn, as we began our group walk over the Brooklyn Bridge, ending with a reception at the offices of C. Virginia Fields, Borough President of Manhattan. The Chat 'n' Chew Network was introduced at the Symposium. Through this Network veteran AASWG members facilitated three forums for informal exchange among participants at the beginning, middle, and end of the Symposium.

Contents of This Volume

Opening Chapters

Our hope is that this volume builds on the sense of connection engendered by the symposium, and engages readers in our effort to extend the reach and quality of social work with groups. Certainly the two keynote papers included in the first section of this book open that possibility. Robert Salmon and Roselle Kurland's address, "Caught in the Doorway between Education and Practice: Group Work's Battle for Survival," brought participants to the edge of their seats as they considered the challenges to group work's survival. Their paper provides fuel for new resolve to *Think Group* and engage others in that process. Darlyne Bailey's presentation, focusing on the essential nature of groups in community social work practice, provided essential tools to use a group frame of reference as we approach professional practice and community development. Her paper with Nina Aranoff, "Thinking Group in Collaboration and Community Building: An Interprofessional Model," brings readers an evolutionary perspective and contemporary perspectives in using this way of thinking. These initial chapters are followed by sections focused on social work education for practice with groups, group work as with adults, and a final section focusing on group work with children.

Education for Social Work Practice with Groups

Traditionally, education for social work practice with groups has blended theory, practice expertise, and research to address the concerns of clients and other constituents, to understand how change occurs, and to help students and professional social workers acquire and enhance the knowledge and skills essential for group work practice. To enable group work to sustain itself as a potent and vital practice modality, educators and practitioners must embrace this tripartite approach to social group work practice and education as they develop, apply, and evaluate innovative approaches to social work education for practice with groups. Several presenters at the 24th Symposium took the challenge of the Symposium's theme to heart: They "thought group," and they created stimulating workshops and presentations that addressed educational challenges faced in both field instruction and classroom settings.

In his chapter, George Getzel uses Schon's (1987) ideas about "reflection-in-action" to critically analyze the cross-generational transmission of group work skills and to identify failures in group work education. He concludes with some "modest proposals" to strengthen group work education, including more parity between field instruction and classroom teaching and the more effective use of "group work practice laboratories" to demonstrate group work *in vivo*.

Middleman and Wood's (1990) dictum to "think group" applies equally well to broader community level educational efforts. By "thinking group" we bring to life C. Wright Mills's charge to see beyond a series of individual cases (1943) and to understand the confluence of "private troubles" and "public issues." Only by understanding the essential connection between the challenges individuals face and societal responses can we appreciate the needs of people and their impinging environments and develop solutions that will benefit society and all of its citizens. Virginia Strand and her colleagues discuss how identifying mutual concerns an innovative "town and gown" partnership between human service organizations and schools of social work to support the professionalization and stabilization of the child welfare workforce was developed. The collaboration they describe is an excellent example of the value of group work principles for task groups addressing larger societal concerns.

Arielle Dylan continues the discussion of "mutuality" in her stimulating chapter on "mutual empathy." She speculates about reasons for empathic failure by professionals when they encounter marginalized, low-income, and addicted clients. She proposes an innovative staff development program that addresses the failures and promotes mutual empathy. Mark Doel's chapter concludes this section. Drawing on findings from an action research project, he explores a holistic approach to assessing group work practice and draws implications for continuing professional development.

Group Work with Adults

The post-9/11 period demonstrated the need of persons to reach out to each other. Group work has always recognized the power of thinking group to address the service needs of persons. Marchini's chapter discusses how group work was used to support individual firefighters assigned to work with the families of firefighters who died at the twin towers. The intensity of providing the families with both resources and emotional support takes a personal tool. Thus these individuals were brought together in a group to provide them with the emotional support needed and a place where knowledge of existing resource could be shared. The chapter highlights how context, specifically the mutual aid tradition among firefighters and an atmosphere of crisis, can lead to an accelerated movement through the phases of group development.

The ability of groups to challenge social isolation is highlighted in the Slaght chapter which discusses a voluntary community-based group designed to help women in their transition from the stigmatized position of welfare recipient to employment. The reality burdens of single motherhood and low self-esteem were addressed through the emotional support, support for individual growth, and the sharing of knowledge about resources possible in the group process. Further the authors describe how the group provided opportunities for self-actualization through collective pressuring of the community to provide additional needed resources.

Lordan, Quirke, and Wilson focus their chapter on the value of the activity of mask making. They discuss how mask making can be used to help group members deconstruct received wisdom and construct new knowledge. In the act of mask making one member acts on another in a way that requires trust and an acceptance of powerlessness. Reflections about this process provide members learning opportunities. The authors are aware that this activity, like many others, include dilemmas which must be considered before committing oneself to the use of the technique with a given population.

Group Work with Children and Youth

Malekoff, using stories and poetry, explores the question of why group workers who work with children do not command the respect they deserve. He points out that too often group work with children is equated with noisy, fun activities run by persons who do not dress like a "professional." Thus all too often the depth of the work taking place is not recognized. Malekoff alerts us to the essence of the work and challenges all group workers to support each other to continue their important work with children.

Subsequent chapters demonstrate the importance of groups to meeting the needs of children and youth. Mullin and Langosch address the issue of death in their chapter on a 12-week group addressed to the needs of children exposed to the death of a caretaker. Highlighted is the way the group worker can address the symptoms of intrusive memories, hyper-arousal, avoidance and numbing, common among such children, through the use of art, Cognitive Behavioral techniques and stress reduction training. The atmosphere of safety and affect competency provided by the group experience enabled positive change.

Driscoll and Fadelici point out how relational issues and social isolation are common among adolescent sexual offenders who ultimately use an unacceptable method to meet a valid need. The authors describe how group work can facilitate connection between "the otherness" and the self in a way that develops empathy and prevents sexual abuse of others.

Summary

In closing, this volume provides a broad view of what scholars from wide range fields of practice are *thinking* about social work with groups. It is with pride that the works of the contributing authors' are presented, and with sadness that it has taken so long to reach the large numbers of social group work practitioners, educators, and students who will find their work of great value.

References

Abels, S. L. & Abels, P. (1981). *Social work with groups: Proceedings 1987 Symposium*. Louisville, KY: Committee for the Advancement of Social Work with Groups.

Cohen, C. S. (1993). *Enhancing social group work opportunities in field work education*. Dissertation, City University of New York.

Elliott, Stuart (1998). Apple endorses some achievers who "think different." *New York Times* (Aug. 3). D1, 7.

Fanney, V. (2003). AASWG Symposium sessions open interdisciplinary paths. *Social Work Education Reporter, 51*(1), 4, 41.

Hirayama, H. & Hirayama, K. (1986). Empowerment through group participation: Process and goal. In M. Parnes (Ed.), *Innovations in social group work: Feedback from practice to theory: Proceedings of the Annual Group Work Symposium* (pp. 119–132). New York, London: The Haworth Press.

Johnson, D. W. & Johnson, F. P. (2000). *Joining together: Group theory and group skills* (7th ed.). Boston: Allyn & Bacon.

Lowy, L. (1955). *Adult education and group work*. New York: Whiteside, Inc., and William Morrow & Co.

Mills, C. W. (1943). The professional ideology of social pathologists. *American Journal of Sociology, 49*(2), 165–180.

Mills, C. W. (1959). *The sociological imagination*. New York: Oxford University Press.

Ono, Yumiko. (1997). Apple is trying a "different" image polish, *Wall Street Journal*, no. 203 (Oct. 10, 1977), B8.

Middleman, R. R. & Wood, G. G. (1990). *Skills for Direct Practice in Social Work*. New York: Columbia University Press.

Schon, D. A. (1987). *Educating the reflective practitioner*. San Francisco: Jossey-Bass.

Schwartz, W. (1971). On the use of groups in social work practice. In William Schwartz and Serapio R. Zalba (Eds.), *The Practice of Group Work*. (pp. 3–24). New York: Columbia University Press.

Steinberg, D. (1997). *The Mutual-Aid Approach to Working with Groups*. Northvale, NJ: Jason Aronson, 1977.

Sundel, M., Glasser, P., Sarri, R., & Vinter, R. (Eds.). (1985). *Individual change through small groups* (2nd ed.). New York: Free Press.

1 Caught in the Doorway Between Education and Practice

Group Work's Battle for Survival[1]

Robert Salmon and Roselle Kurland

Ten years ago we presented a plenary paper at the Atlanta symposium of the Association for the Advancement of Social Work with Groups titled *Making Joyful Noise: Presenting, Promoting, and Portraying Group Work to and for the Profession*. We started that presentation with a famous line from Shakespeare's King Henry the Fifth, "Once more unto the breach, dear friends, once more; or close the wall up with our English dead!" (1918, p. 40). The intent of Henry's speech was to rouse his vastly outnumbered forces in the forthcoming battle with the French. The purpose of Henry's speech was achieved: the English were successful. They survived. They won.

The analogy we made to Henry was intentional. Group work was—and is—a vastly outnumbered method minority in social work, and we were in an intense struggle to maintain social work with groups as a viable part of social work. Our paper discussed history, problems and issues, and presented ideas about what we needed to do to preserve it.

A decade has gone by since that presentation, an appropriate time to ask how have we done in the past ten years. In what direction is the profession moving? How has the method fared in education and in practice? How are new graduates with interest in group work received, and what problems do they face as new professionals?

To continue the analogy to Henry, we can say, with assuredness, that we have *not* won. The struggle for group work's survival continues and our concern is that we are losing the battle. The profession and the method face even more serious issues than those they confronted ten years ago.

To understand the predicament in which group work and social work practitioners with particular interest in and commitment to group work find themselves, three areas need to be looked at. First, there is the lack of group work education in schools of social work and the implications for practice of that lack. Second, there are the ways in which research is currently being emphasized in our profession. And third, there are conditions, particularly

1   An abbreviated version of this presentation appears in the newsletter, *Stand-Punkt: Social; Hamburger Forum für Soziale Arbeit*, 1/2005, translated into German by Jürgen Kalcher.

funding requirements, in many agencies that militate against good group work practice.

The lack of group work education in schools of social work has been well documented (see, for example, Kurland & Salmon, 1996; Middleman, 1992; Parry, 1995). Very few social work schools offer more than one course in group work practice. Frequently, such courses are taught by teachers who, themselves, do not know social group work very well. The may teach work with groups but not social group work. A recent study (Strozier, 1997) found that even with the existence of many solid group work textbooks, by far the most used text in group work courses in schools of social work was Irvin Yalom's *The Theory and Practice of Group Psychotherapy*. That is a fine book, certainly, but social group work and group psychotherapy are *not* synonymous.

The lack of group work education results in a premium being placed in practice on speed of group formation. When new workers say they need time for planning, to assess need, to get to know potential members, to give potential members a chance to get a sense of them, they are dismissed: "Oh, that's the stuff you get in school. This is the real world. We don't have time for that here." How sad! The lack of group work education results in too many social workers who have never learned the connection between planning and meaningful, successful groups.

The lack of education also results in too many social workers who do not appreciate such crucial concepts as mutual aid, stages of group development and their implications for practice, the value and importance of conflict in a group (Steinberg, 1993), the use of activity, and the difference between group work and casework in a group (Kurland & Salmon, 1992). All these have been described elsewhere and so we will not dwell on them here.

The lack of group work education has also resulted in an abundance and every-growing number of curriculum-driven groups. These are not groups that have a *suggested* curriculum. They are not curriculum-*based* groups. Rather they are curriculum-DRIVEN groups with pre-set content that is to be applied without flexibility and according to a pre-determined timetable. They are called groups, but these are not social work groups. Perhaps they might be called classes, but actually they are not good classes either.

Communication in such groups is leader-directed with minimal interaction among group members. Member strengths and mutual aid are not elicited or emphasized. Leaders of such groups are instructed to stay with the curriculum, not to deviate from it even when a member wants to discuss a concern that is relevant but not on the agenda. "Sorry, we don't have time for that. We need to move on."

We believe that such groups have become increasingly popular because the group work understanding and skill that are needed to develop, guide, and utilize group process, and to maximize relationships and mutual aid among group members are just not being taught today. A set curriculum may be a way to overcome the deficit; it may even be comforting at first to the worker.

But such curricula soon become counter-productive and stifling. They leave no room for innovation, for creativity, for individualization.

A few weeks ago, as classes were just beginning, a student in my group work class approached me to make sure that the group she would be leading was an acceptable part of her field work assignment. This student is an administration major with a minor in group work and, as such, is required to work with at least one group. She described a curriculum-*driven* group on parenting for women heads-of-households in the shelter where she worked. I made a face. She quickly picked up on that, "I'm doing another group," she said. She described a residents' council at the shelter that aims to empower residents and to enhance neighborliness among a diverse resident population (elderly men and women, single men and women with HIV or AIDS, women with young children). In describing this group, she demonstrated an effervescence that seemed absent in her description of the curriculum group. She was, herself, excited at the opportunities that this group provided for creative practice. My response to this alternative was enthusiastic. I made another face, the opposite of my first. She quickly responded, "My director thought that that group wouldn't be acceptable, that it wouldn't meet the requirements for school—that it had to be a group with a curriculum." What is group work becoming?

Simultaneous with the rise of curriculum-driven groups has been the ascendancy of *techniques* to replace the group work method. We believe that this is also a direct result of the lack of social group work education. In New York City, for example, a "semi-profession"—that of Youth Worker—has been identified from which social work has been excluded or is, at best, a minimal part. The knowledge, understanding, and skill that social workers bring to work with youth are unrecognized. Youth workers are being used to staff the majority of the extensive Beacon School programs throughout the City. Though a great deal of their work is with children in groups, the training these youth workers receive for this job too often consists of techniques that are not rooted in principled understanding of group work practice. Similarly, other styles or what might be called "models" of practice with groups have arisen that reflect almost no knowledge of social group work.

What is taking place today is that a premium is being place on whatever works, on what have come to be called "best practices." Though some of these best practices are good techniques that may even be quite creative, the lack of knowledge and understanding with which they are applied means that they are limited and one-dimensional. Harold Lewis said that techniques "are often attractive to those liking for facile solutions to difficult problems in uncertain situations" (1982, p. 167). But, Lewis added, they do not reflect the years of experience, experiment, discovery, and intervention that make up the knowledge, purpose, values, and professional sanction of a *method* of practice. Techniques are simply not enough. Yet the lack of group work education has resulted in practitioners who seem desperate to jump on any techniques that they are able to find.

The ascendance of research and the effects that arise present another problem that confronts our profession in general and group work in particular. Research is important. It has the potential to increase our knowledge of client needs and social situations, of practice interventions, and of program effectiveness. Perhaps even more importantly, it encourages us to discipline our thinking and to sharpen our decision-making acumen.

But research today is becoming too often not a way to learn but rather a way to prove. The rise of research has its roots in the halls of academia. It is being used today in a battle for professional status and prestige, to demonstrate to the academic bestowers of promotion and tenure that social workers are not "soft," that their rigor is beyond question. To demonstrate that, a premium is being placed on quantitative research. Qualitative research is given a much less preferred standing.

Such an emphasis in academia has put the teaching of practice "on the back burner" in many schools of social work (Hartman, 1990). It has resulted in proposals to accept students into doctoral programs without a hiatus in their educational path to allow time for experience in direct practice (O'Neill, 2000). Such proposals would make the primary aim of doctoral education the production of skillful researchers who may have knowledge *about* practice, but who do not have knowledge gained through the experience of actual practice. Such proposals have enormous negative implications for the quality of the teaching of practice in our schools.

With the effort to use research to establish social work's status and to prove its professional legitimacy has come an ever-deepening chasm between research and practice, and the usefulness of research to social work practitioners. The ascent of research that is taking place in social work today threatens to make quality practice obsolete. It places a premium on practice that emphasizes the quickly measurable and demonstrable. It too often fails to take into account the complexities of individuals and of the relationship between the individual and the social. Such complexity is often not meaningfully measurable. Evidence is not always immediately available, for example, to prove the value of the kinds of socialization groups with youths, so much a part of group work practice, whose significance and benefits may be realized over time and even years after their occurrence.

Professional judgment in social work practice is being devalued as a result of the emphasis on research. Recently I taught a professional seminar course at Hunter to students in our one-year residence program, students who have had substantial experience in social work before coming to school. In this course, which takes place in their last semester of school, students are asked to write a paper of quality in an area of their interest that is rooted in their own practice. At the start of the course, each student discusses the subject of her interest.

One student, describing her interest, explained that she has been working for the past eight years with families with young children with learning disabilities. She had noticed a problem that she would like to examine in her paper. "When a child is very young, the services and resources for a family are plentiful and individualized," she said. "But when the child reaches the age of five, the locus of service becomes the Board of Education and services become less plentiful and are delivered in a more bureaucratic, less individualized, and more stigmatizing way. This creates difficulties and stress for the family." She was proposing a paper that would discuss this transition and the difficulties for families it presented.

I thought her subject was an excellent one. "How do you envision yourself going about it?" I asked. "I'd put together a focus group of parents and ask them what difficulties they'd faced when their children turned five," she replied. "But don't you have a good idea of what those difficulties are based on your eight years of work with the families?" I said. "Seems to me you want to be *examining* the difficulties in your paper, not just *identifying* them." "Yes, I know what the difficulties are," she responded, "but in research we were taught that we shouldn't impose our thinking, that it needed to come from the clients."

This student's perception of what research is saying is, in fact, an erroneous one. But regardless of its veracity, that is the sense with which our students are emerging from social work school. We have seen that perception demonstrated over and over again by graduating students, that their experience does not count and is not to be trusted. The result, we believe, is a social work discourse that is becoming devoid of thoughtful discussion, one in which no ideas are valid unless they have been poked and prodded and examined in formal research studies. Increasingly, less and less room exists for practice wisdom and professional judgment. To eliminate such wisdom and judgment is to deprive workers and the profession itself of the excitement and vast benefits of experience.

It is difficult to practice group work in many agencies today. The lack of group work education and the emphasis on research contribute to the difficulty. In addition, funding sources and managed care often place a premium on numbers served, on rapid improvement, on time limits, and on concrete goals that can be measured easily. Such emphases can place constraints upon and make difficult the formation of groups that are meaningful to their members.

One new worker in a community health clinic noticed that the agency was working individually with a number of teenage girls who were survivors of childhood sexual abuse. She thought that a group for these young women would make sense. But her suggestion was met with discouragement, as she explained:

> I had thought that a weekly group in addition to individual meetings on a weekly basis would make sense, but [the director] told me that this would not fare well. She said that the treatment goal for those seeking help at the agency was that the level of care should be stepped down over the course of a client's treatment. And if I were to have group meetings

for these girls, in addition to their weekly scheduled individual sessions, it would appear that they were needing more, not less, care. The result would be that questions would automatically be asked about whether the clients were actually deteriorating in their ability to function, as it would seem that they were requiring more, not less, attention.

The group this worker suggested never did get formed.

Neither did a group for a similar population that another worker, also in a mental health clinic, thought about trying to start. But in this instance, it was the worker herself who aborted the formation of the group because of concerns that she had. "There is a tendency in the agency to open up groups and 'broaden' the theme when there is not enough attendance," she said. She cited a group for isolated elderly persons that was opened to younger disabled clients when only a few older persons attended, even though the elderly clients attended consistently and the group seemed to be meeting their needs. "I can imagine some similarities between the isolation of elderly and of younger disabled clients," she said, "but I think that mixing these two rather different groups demonstrated an insensitivity to each."

The concern this worker had about forming a group for teenage girls who had been sexually abused was that since the number of such girls being served by the agency was small, she would be asked eventually by the agency to open the group to other populations to increase the number of members—male survivors of sexual abuse, perhaps, or adult survivors. She thought that such a request would be inappropriate. As a result, she did not even attempt to form the group. She did not wish to risk the professional conflict that such a request would raise for her.

In elementary schools, another setting where groups have been used traditionally, group work has also become increasingly difficult. The emphasis on test scores has made all too many public schools oppressive places that lack any sense of joy or fun or creativity. Teachers feel extremely pressured to elicit from their students a good performance on standardized tests. School administrators' purposes for groups often conflict with the purposes of school social workers.

The principal of one elementary school, for example, wanted the school newspaper group and the product it produced to be a "show piece" that she could use to demonstrate her school's excellence. She banned two boys from continuing to participate in the newspaper group, even over the objections of the social worker who led the group. She told the social worker that the boys had been noisy and that they needed to behave and demonstrate self-control before they could be allowed to participate. She was adamant about her decision, even when the social worker attempted to explain her point of view about the benefits of the group for these boys, whose group participation had been active and enthusiastic.

The current climate makes it difficult for social workers in schools because so often they have a different perspective from the teachers, whose emphasis is on better test scores and classroom management and control. The following example, reported by a social work student whose internship was in an elementary school, illustrates that different perspective:

> When I arrived in the cafeteria there was an excited buzz among the teachers. The stop light that had been ordered for the cafeteria had arrived and the teachers felt this was a long overdue addition to help control the noise level. Previously they had relied on making the children stand against the wall when they spoke above a whisper. Now the stop light would be used instead to do the monitoring. It was promptly mounted on the wall of the cafeteria. If the kids were quiet, the light was green. If they started to get noisy, the light turned yellow. And if they got too loud, it turned red and a piercing alarm went off. I asked a ten-year-old girl what she thought about the stoplight and she said it made her feel like a car. (Giambalvo, 2001)

Too often in schools today, the connection between students' emotional health and their educational performance is unappreciated. And the role that group work might play in fostering both is similarly unrecognized. That makes group work in schools difficult.

Not so long ago, to be a social worker with special commitment to group work placed one in a supportive and stimulating community of colleagues, teachers, supervisors and mentors who shared common values, understanding, and excitement about group work practice. The method was celebrated and vibrant. That is no longer true today. Those with particular interest in work with groups find it difficult to locate colleagues, teachers, supervisors, and mentors with depth of knowledge, understanding, and skill who can appreciate, support, and animate their group work efforts.

To be a group worker today is to be lonely. As Emily Wolff Newman, a recent graduate, has described:

> It is very isolating to be a social group worker today. Social group work is a method of practice that seems to be a whisper if at all audible in most graduate school programs. As a result, there are few people trained in social group work and those of us who are, are the odd birds of our agencies. We are nearly surrounded by colleagues who share a similar social group work philosophy or understanding. (Newmann, 2000)

Another recent graduate described her work experience in this way:

> I am now facilitating four groups I created, two with displaced World Trade Center workers/survivors and two with teens in foster care. I love the group work but it is also a very isolated business with almost no peers and a huge lack of understanding and support. The agency, also, has terrible ethics . . . it seeks public relations and dollars, often to the

detriment of clients and workers. Because of this, as well as lack of almost any supervision, I will be looking for other work.

The loneliness that recent graduates feel should not come as a surprise. A quarter of a century ago, Emanuel Tropp (1978) asked, "What happened to group work?" He discussed how the rise of generic training and education resulted in a decreasing pool of qualified practitioners, consultants, and educators in group work, as well as the virtual disappearance of articles about group work. He urges us then to put group work back into social work.

Then a dozen years ago, Ruth Middleman summarized the situation powerfully when she said:

> Social work is choking these days . . . for all practical and practice purposes; [it] has coughed-out teaching basic group practice know-how from its core, from the required foundation knowledge, even in today's times when groups have emerged as a major modality in service delivery. And this leaves the graduate open to varieties of contamination, infection, and defection. Social work educations vital signs signal DANGER. A quick upward thrust to its belly is needed to revive knowledgeable social work with groups. (Middleman, 1992, p. 16)

And then, two years ago, when Hunter's School of Social Work was being visited for reaccreditation, our group work sequence was singled out for particular praise by the site team. But one concerned team member looked at our faculty, all of whom are of senior status, and asked a pointed and poignant and very loud and resounding question: "What is going to happen to group work when your current faculty leave? Will it continue?" There is good reason for concern. If the teachers disappear, inevitably and ultimately the practitioners will disappear also.

We see group work's current situation as one of crisis. We need to act now in regard to the lack of group work education, the emphases of research, and the agency conditions that we have described here today. If we do not, it will not take even 25 years more before group work will disappear. There are no easy solutions.

It is important, certainly, that we encourage young practitioners to teach group work and to consider a teaching career. At Hunter, a school that has maintained method specializations, a recent curriculum change requiring students to take a second method resulted in an abundance of group work classes being requested. To meet that demand, we hired five of our own recent graduates to teach group work as adjunct instructors. Their enthusiasm and excitement was wonderful. The response of the students in their classes was extremely positive. A key ingredient in their success was the support offered to these new teachers by experienced faculty. They were not treated as adjuncts typically are, not left to sink or swim on their own. Rather, we had regular sequence meetings to discuss group work and teaching, to support their efforts and encourage the new and creative approaches they wanted to try. Such efforts to develop the scholars and teachers of group work's future are crucial.

Above all, group work educators and practitioners must work together to prevent the disappearance of group work. Neither can address the crisis alone. Referring to the growing gap and increasingly disparate goals that she was seeing between educators and practitioners, Ann Hartman urged their coming together to address complex social problems and challenges. "The profession must draw together," she said. "Educators and practitioners need to collaborate, share their expertise and support each other in the achievement of the profession's mission" (1990, p. 44). We concur. We know of no better place for such collaboration to occur than AASWG, an organization which brings together educators and practitioners. Our Association needs to develop an organized campaign to assure group work's survival.

AASWG needs to develop NOW a strategic plan to be carried out over the next five years. Such a plan needs to involve a collaborative effort of social workers at all levels—educators, agency executives, line workers—who share an appreciation and respect for group work. One ingredient of such a plan might be a series of meetings with executives of programs—the Beacon school program is one example—where social group work's approach needs to be used but is underrepresented. We need to emphasize to them the importance and potential usefulness of bringing group work into their programs.

In the past, AASWG's efforts have gone toward many needs in a myriad of directions. It has been concerned, as well, with its own survival. Now it is group work's survival that must become paramount. To actively engage in and lead such a campaign might simultaneously strengthen both our method and our own organization.

And so we end as we started by saying to you, "Once more unto the breach, dear friends."

References

Giambalvo, S. (2001). *Lessons from the field: The need for collaborative process and planning in school social work.* (Unpublished Paper), Hunter College School of Social Work.

Hartman, A. (1990). Education for direct practice. *Families in Society, 71*(1), 44–50.

Kurland, R. & Salmon, R. (1992). Group work vs. casework in a group: Implications for teaching and practice. *Social Work with Groups, 15*(4), 19–32.

Kurland, R. & Salmon, R. (1996). Making joyful noise: Presenting, promoting and portraying group work to and for the profession. In B. Stempler & M. Glass (Eds.), *Social group work today and tomorrow* (pp. 19–32). New York: The Haworth Press.

Lewis, H. (1982). *The intellectual base of social work practice.* New York: The Haworth Press.

Middleman, R. R. (1992). Group work and the Heimlich maneuver: Unchoking social work education. In D. F. Fike & B. Rittner (Eds.), *Working from strengths: The essence of group work* (pp. 16–39). Miami, FL: Center for Group Work Studies.

Newmann, E. W. (2000). Pearls in the muck. *Social Work with Groups, 23*(3), 19–36.

O'Neill, J. V. (2000). Few social workers follow path to Ph.D. *NASW News, 45*(0), 3.

Parry, J. K (1995). Social group work, sink or swim: Where is group work in a generalist curriculum? In M. O. Feit, J. H. Ramey, J. S. Wodarski & A. R. Mann (Eds.), *Capturing the power of diversity* (pp. 23–39). New York: The Haworth Press.

Shakespeare, W. (1918). *The Life of King Henry the Fifth*, III, 1, 2, R. D. French (Ed.), New Haven: Yale University Press.

Steinberg, D. (1993). Some findings from a study on the impact of group work education on social work practitioners' work with groups. *Social Work with Groups, 16*(3), 23–39.

Strozier, A. L. (1997). Group work education: What is being taught? *Social Work with Groups, 20*(1), 65–77.

Tropp, E. (1978). Whatever happened to group work? *Social Work with Groups, 1*(1), 85–94.

2 Thinking Group in Collaboration and Community Building

An Interprofessional Model[1]

Nina L. Aronoff and Darlyne Bailey

Our profession of social work builds on a long practice tradition of relying on collaborative relationships to enhance outcomes for clients, most especially in work with families, groups, organizational teams, and interorganizational alliances within and between communities. Additionally, partnering *across* disciplines builds on a long intellectual tradition in social work in which we have integrated theory from a number of disciplines while developing our own utilization of it. Whether were working with families, organizational teams, or even interorganizational units, the common foundation under-pinning *all* these practice models is the theory and tools of small group work *or* what our symposium will be referring to over the next several days as "think group." Now, more then ever, we are called on to apply and enhance the knowledge and skills inherent in these groups, looking for traditional as well as innovative opportunities. One of the key opportunities in this regard is the interprofessional group as one form of group work that fosters community building. My remarks this morning are intended to affirm those of you that are "interprofessional believers" and welcome the rest of you into a world that knows that social work's mission to improve the human condi-tion can today best be achieved through creating, nurturing, and sustaining small groups comprised of individuals from multiple *professional* back-grounds as well as *consumers* from our local communities.

Small Groups in Social Work: Tradition and History

Work with small groups has historically been one of social work's most powerful tools for understanding and maximizing change, utilizing different types of groups to achieve a variety of purposes. These have been short- and long-term groups, open-ended and single session groups, and groups with a broad range of agendas and style. Though social work with small groups has had varying levels of popularity over time, as evidenced by this international

---

1   Please know that this chapter is part of a larger manuscript, *Interprofessional Small Groups: Building a Tradition*, authored by Nina L. Aronoff and Darlyne Bailey.

symposium it has been a *sustained* method of choice, with many creative applications (see, for example, Gitterman & Shulman, 1994). It is an area of practice that still has great utility and even particular relevance in these times of dealing with issues of greater psycho-social and political complexity. A quick walk through the history and philosophy of social work with small groups will make this assertion even clearer.

Group work evolved out of, and has been sustained by, a recognition that we human beings naturally have a social hunger, a desire for affiliation, and that this hunger can be mobilized for the purposes of individual, group, organization, community, or societal change. Some of the earliest group work came out of the Settlement Movement, with its focus on intervention for the purposes of individual and collective change and an overarching emphasis on democratic values (Lee & Swenson, 1994). This model for group work was largely based on awareness of the individual in the context of the socio-economic pressures of a new industrial culture in the United States, as well as the social justice issues involved in the integration of many new peoples into American society and its emerging social problems. I refer to this as the "first tradition" in social work's use of groups, more commonly known as the *social goals* model. The concurrency of the settlement, recreation, and progressive education movements (p. 417) resulted in what Lee and Swenson describe as value placed on "the importance of belonging, of community, of collective action for the collective good" (p. 418).

The purpose of this first tradition was not only to combat the isolation experienced as a result of individual and collective alienation, but also to address the social goals and development of individuals and communities in the new, multiethnic urban society. The role of the worker in this transition followed the essential values it expressed—to support the mobilization of the inherent forces present in a supportive group context, which is to reciprocate, to help each other. The model was based largely on the writings of prominent social work thinkers like Coyle, Konopka and others (Papell & Rothman, 1966, p. 67). And while it has been criticized by some for its lack of theoretical strength (Garvin & Ephross, 1991), it still garners much respect for its relevancy today.

The second tradition in social work with groups bears out the other side of a tension in social work that also goes back to the early days of the profession; one that stems from an emphasis on social casework (Papell & Rothman, 1966). Based on social work theory, ego psychology, and other theories, what is commonly known as the *remedial* model developed out of a recognition that the group was an effective tool for restoring or rehabilitating individuals (p. 70), using the power of the group to reinforce socialization norms or, if need be, *re-socialize*. While it still relied on the particular mobilizing qualities of the group, it was a departure from the social goals model, moving away from reciprocity between self and society and towards locating the problem in *the individual* and seeking change there. This model's orientation was to the group "as a tool or context" for individual change through a group process rather than the collective growth of the group itself (Papell & Rothman, 1966, p. 71). The worker in this model was decidedly more directive, acting more as a "change agent" (p. 71), helping the participants focus on an individual's change *within* the group in order to be more socially comfortable or, in other words, to better align with the social norms.

With the advent of the civil rights and other empowerment movements of the 1960s, yet a third tradition took hold in social work with groups. Moving back in the direction of combining an individual focus with a more collective one, social work began to adopt a more egalitarian and empowerment-based model of group work, one that relied on the power of group process as a vehicle for personal and interpersonal change through an environment of reciprocity or *mutual aid*.

While this tenet was presented in the earlier social goals model, it became central and far more developed, owing much to the work of our colleagues Schwartz and later Gitterman and Shulman (1994). This model of mutual aid achieved its goals through interpersonal interaction in a supportive context, with emphasis on the elements of identification with others, and normalization and validation of personal and collective issues. The worker in this model had a less demonstrative role, applying the skills of empathy through "tuning in" and responding to members (and self) in order to build and maintain a climate of trust for the purposes of supporting the work of the group (Shulman, 1994). The worker was more of a supporter of group goals and mediator of the relationship between the individuals and their engagement in the group (Shulman & Gitterman, 1994, p. 20). Almost an "ideal group member," the worker helped the group members help each other through refocusing on the group's own goals and development, and through establishing common ground, searching for obstacles to process and reaching for members' and the group's capacity to change (Shulman, 1992, p. 9).

With all that being said still, there are new group work opportunities on the horizon, opportunities for which social work is ideally poised to take a lead role, if we can continue to be as creative in our formulations and applications as we have been historically. In this we can engage in both a spirit of rediscovery as well as discovery, which, as Schwartz has pointed out (in Lee & Swenson, 1994, p. 413), is not always separable and is also a habit toward which professions are naturally inclined.

Interprofessionalism: A Group Approach

Ironically, the new group work opportunities are in part born from the complexity of issues that currently exist in our social environment that collectively signal the need for a yet broader range of responsibility and choices for the helping professions. Individual, family, organizational, and community life are increasingly multifaceted and, often, multi-stressed. This environment calls on all helping professions to consider services from a more contextual, or ecological, point of view. It is a climate in which the search for more positive outcomes must draw on every possible resource for change. And as the social climate is becoming necessarily more *inter-related*, it serves as the perfect midwife to help birth a new "fourth tradition" in group work, one we call interprofessionalism.

Going beyond the multidisciplinary team, and even the most thoughtfully constructed organizational alliance, the goal of the interprofessional model of practice is better outcomes through intersystemic partnering at every level of treatment and evaluation. This approach to practice potentially weaves together some of the best aspects of the group work models described earlier in a creative, dialogic process. The strength of this approach is not just an *additive* measure of practice perspectives and techniques, as is more the case with the multidisciplinary team. In terms of knowledge development the real advantage of the interprofessional group is one of *synergistic* effects. It engages a process that recognizes that individuals are best served by a *range* of professionals, working together and in conjunction with consumers in collaborative relationships (Hooper-Briar & Lawson, 1996). It is also based on the acknowledgement of a common stake—the health and well-being of children, families, organizations, and communities—a paradigm in which creative partnerships are, as our colleagues Corrigan and Bishop report, "a necessity and an obligation of professional leadership" (1997, p. 149).

Let me clarify these terms further. The term *inter-* or *multidisciplinary* can be defined as persons who are discipline-based and focused yet through those lenses work together on a common problem. The implication is that each discipline has its own information and claims and can therefore share them. In relation to the multidisciplinary team, the interprofessional group does need a facilitator of some kind, but the intent of the interprofessional group is not necessarily for that person to represent a difference from others in terms of power and control. The interprofessional group goes further in its scope of integrating partners, by including consumers at every stage of the process, motivated by consumer-defined need, and by expanding the context of involvement beyond a particular site to include a community, region, or even larger geographic locale.

In relation to interorganizational alliances, the interprofessional group shows clear parallels, in terms of having a convener/facilitator and in terms of recognizing the importance of clarifying purpose, membership, phase of development, and level of integration in the group, as well as maximizing the effects of mutual aid. It is not, however, as likely as a strategic alliance to emerge from one of the motivators that are defined more by organizational and less by consumer need; that is, the interprofessional group is not likely to be motivated by domain influence, for example, unless that goal of influence is to achieve consumer-defined change. The interprofessional group actually *depends* on close consumer involvement, whereas the multidisciplinary team and the strategic alliance do not necessarily rely on that factor. Overall, when interprofessional groups are constituted on the basis of responding to a valid, current social service need, they are akin to *all* the social group work models—

from the individual and social orientation of the first tradition social goals model, to the second tradition remedial model and its concentration on socialization, and to the third tradition mutual aid model centered on the concepts of mutuality and reciprocity as conducive environmental factors for change: traditions all grounded in a sense of the value of group process and development.

There's yet another term that is worth clarifying in relation to interprofessionalism and that is *boundary spanning*. This process refers to representatives from one or more systems that have functioning roles in other systems, while not departing from their orienting perspective. This exchange of claims, moreover, allows disciplines to remain separate and bounded and still benefit from the results of each one's focused approach, possibly opening new arenas for any one of them.

The term *interprofessional* goes beyond this definition. In the interprofessional group, there is *an openness to the influence of others* and the group as a whole, based in the intention *to build an environment of co-creation*. This is an environment committed to a productive synergy, a kind of "mutual aid plus." It requires both a firm grounding in one's profession *and* an ability to be flexible in regard to role, manifestation of skills, control, and level of separateness. In regard to this last issue, for some folks the most challenging feature of the interprofessional group may be the willingness to relinquish a definite separateness not only from other professions but *also* from *consumers*. In the interprofessional group, any and all members are potentially experts, including the consumer or consumer group from which the group's purpose is generated. In this environment, all are asked to stretch, to dynamically embrace the concepts of partnership, mutual aid, and social responsibility on an expanded and expansive level.

Drawing from the recent literature in this area (Corrigan & Bishop, 1997; Hogan, 1996; Hooper-Briar & Lawson, 1996; Zlotnik et al., 1999), *interprofessionalism* describes a process involving persons of a range of affiliations, together serving common goals of service planning and delivery. It implies a flexibility of professional boundaries that allows for a highly interactive process of knowledge, skill, and role exchange. Most importantly it is more inclusive and participatory, in that it involves *all* stakeholders, including consumers along with professionals.

In this way, interprofessionalism goes *beyond boundary spanning to be a boundary synergizing* paradigm that when carefully constructed and enacted can lead to building community among all involved. Additionally, interprofessionalism enables the group to be actively engaged with the *external* community—an interplay that is critical to social change.

Through this process of interprofessionalism a new dynamic is generated among formerly separate entities, bringing about new ways of conceptualizing and new results. As Graham and Barter (1999) have pointed out, interprofessionalism is not an end in itself but rather a critical tool needed to achieve the changes to which we are committed. It offers a particular framework in which familiar issues (and solutions) can be seen in new ways, and formerly "invisible" issues and solutions can now be seen. In short, interprofessionalism offers a way to integrate collaborative group models at *all* levels of practice, in a single, yet comprehensive, paradigm.

This way of seeing and being is actually not brand new, just little known. In fact the interprofessional framework has been evolving over the past 30 years. The emerging literature on interprofessionalism documents a range of initiatives and models (see, for example, Corrigan & Bishop, 1997; Dryfoos, 1998; Graham & Barter, 1999; Hooper-Briar & Lawson, 1996; Roberts, Rule, & Innocenti, 1998; Zlotnik et al., 1999). We are also seeing schools of social work committing to an integration of interprofessional concepts and opportunities as in the introduction to the mission statement of Wheelock College's Graduate Department of Social Work in Boston, Massachusetts (e.g., Hogan, 1996). Others, like Bryn Mawr in Pennsylvania, offer students the opportunity to include integrative seminars and mentorships in their trainings that are specifically interprofessional in nature with the goal of enhancing their abilities to provide more effective client-based services. Interprofessional practice requires, as School (in Zlotnik et al., 1999) states, "a 'new practitioner' who works more collaboratively and more respectfully with clients, patients, children, youth, and families, and who pushes the boundaries of her or his job description and sees children in the context of families and families in the context of communities" (p. 1). Interprofessional groups, made of practitioners such as these, need to be at their highest functioning in order to achieve these overarching objectives. And social work's foundations in group work, the depth of theory, skills, and experience, ideally support this goal.

With this understanding, let's go further and turn our attention to inter-professionalism in comparison to sound group work principles. We now know that interprofessionalism is a framework within which we can combine our knowledge of small group work, our background with multidisciplinary teams, and our experience with strategic alliances, integrated with a practice and policy agenda that meets the needs of today's complex human service issues. The resulting group model addresses change goals that are consumer-focused, contextually based and holistically oriented, are built on the primacy of valuing partnership and reciprocity, and guided by practice knowledge and success with individuals, groups, organizations, communities, and goals of social change.

As described in our quick walk through history, social work groups have come in a great array of shapes and sizes, a continuum along which inter-professional groups certainly fit. And this is just not a "good enough" fit but an exciting opportunity to explore how our understanding of the social work group enhances our functioning in and development of interprofessional groups (and vice versa). First, there is little in the *theoretical formulations* of small group work that does not apply in the case of interprofessional groups—there is a similar need for an understanding of the importance of *purpose and structure, worker role, stages of development* and the nature of group process throughout. The interprofessional group is similar to the most basic concepts of the third tradition, our mutual aid model, with a renewed version of the social goals model (this time with a stronger theoretical base), in that it has a keen focus on the empowerment of all members, a consumer-centered basis for the work, and a commitment to new models for change based on a collaborative process, in which the goal is to reflexively attend to the group's internal workings as well as to its connections to the external environment.

Looking at the concept of the group in *developmental process*—during the course of each meeting and over the life of the group—interprofessional groups can be seen to function as all small groups do, in comprehensible phases. This, again, reinforces the importance of the need for social workers skilled in small group work to be engaged in this form of practice. Where the interprofessional group falls on the continuum of small groups is among those that are at least facilitator-directed and most group member-driven. One of the key differences from social work groups (including the multidisciplinary team and interorganizational alliances) is seen in terms of *worker role* or *use of self*. In the interprofessional group, there is still a need for a member, or members, to have solid knowledge of group work, with an eye toward understanding members' levels of involvement, the group's purpose, the structure and phases of development, as well as various ways to mobilize the group's forces to manifest the changes it seeks. However, expanding on the mutual aid tradition of being "an ideal group member," the social worker in the interprofessional group applies all of the group work skills without having to be the "leader," yet still emphasizing mutually empowerment-focused process throughout the life of the group. The true leadership is in this empowered group which goes beyond being consumer-*centered* to actually being consumer-*driven*. That is, the identification of need and potential solutions is *defined* by the consumer members and *supported* by a range of professionals.

Conclusion

In sum, social work's body of group work knowledge fills a gap in interprofessionalism—by virtue of our history, we come with the philosophical, theoretical, and skill-based knowledge of practice and research with a great variety of groups. And interprofessionalism also fills a gap in the social group work paradigm. It presents an opportunity to reassert social work skills with groups in an important, and currently evolving, human service trend, and to do so in some new ways. It fits in well to the paradigm of group work as a model of choice, even though the field emphasizes it less now relative to some other periods in our history. We all know that the standard reasons for using groups, which ideally stem from the philosophical principles of good practice, can also come down to a matter of maximizing resources—money, people, time, space, etc. Interprofessional groups meet these standards; and they can also be used to support a renewed focus on group work, its traditions, and its innovations. In many ways this has been shown, including the ways that it represents a return to the broader agenda of community building, social action, and policy development. In this example alone, interprofessional groups represent a reintegration of the social goals model of early group work but with a heightened, contemporary awareness of empowerment issues, in practice *and* in research (Breton, 1990), and our undeniable connection to the global society in which we live. We ignore these opportunities at risk to our consumers. Using an interprofessional lens, we ignore these opportunities at risk to our colleagues, and our students, as well.

The social work vision has always been to intervene in the human condition, wherever and however possible, in order to alleviate suffering, empower the disenfranchised, and to work for social justice, in ways that are client-based and contextually framed. Theses are the cornerstones by which we continue to be guided, and also the basis for renewing claims of legitimation. The question for us as social workers becomes: How do we continue as a productive profession, interfacing our strengths with the demands of the current sociocultural context to produce a new blend of practice that is both innovative and consistent with our mission?

Now more than ever we need creative, systemic thinkers and practitioners. Collectively we must continually redress the persistent emphasis on the individual as the locus of "the presenting problem" and hence, the focus of "treatment." Today we need models to address the issues that connect one traditional area of practice to the next, and one profession to the next, with consumers and other community members. The professions in general, and ourselves included, might do better to focus less on staking claims to the boundaries that identify us *exclusively* and *against* other professions, and focus more on exploring how boundaries, and the implementation of disciplinary practices, need to change to create better programmatic outcomes for consumers, and policies of our global society, through more participatory, integrated, and interprofessional interventions.

To conclude, the time for thinking and behaving inclusively and purposefully is now. And as folks who know the power of groups and the growing challenges in our work, we need only remember the words of Fredrick Buechner (1933, p. 119) that amazing things happen in our work when our "deep gladness meets the world's deep needs."

References

Association for the Advancement of Social Work with Groups, Inc. (2000). *Standards for social work practice with groups*. Akron, OH: AASWG, Inc.

Breton, M. (1990). Learning from social group work traditions. *Social Work with Groups, 13*(3), 21–34.

Buechner, F. (1993). *Wishful thinking: A seeker's ABC*. San Francisco: Harper.

Corrigan, D. & Bishop, K. K. (1997). Creating family-centered integrated service systems and interprofessional educational programs to implement them. *Social Work in Education, 19*(3), 149–163.

Dryfoos, J. G. (1998). *Safe passage: Making it through adolescence in a risky society.* New York: Oxford University Press.

Garvin, C. D. & Ephross, P. H. (1991). Group theory, In R. R. Greene & P. H. Ephross (Eds.), *Human behavior theory and social work practice* (pp. 177–201). New York: Aldine de Gruyter.

Gitterman, A. (1994). Developing a new group service: Strategies and skills. In A. Gitterman & L. Shulman (Eds.), *Mutual aid groups: Vulnerable populations, and the life cycle* (2nd ed.), (pp. 59–80). New York: Columbia University Press.

Gitterman, A. & Shulman, L. (Eds.). (1994) *Mutual aid groups, vulnerable populations, and the life cycle* (2nd ed.). New York: Columbia University Press.

Graham, J. R. & Barter, K. (1999). Collaboration: A social work practice model. *Families in Society, 80*(1), 6–13.

Hogan, P. (1996). Transforming professional education. In K. Hooper-Briar & H. A. Lawson (Eds.), *Expanding partnerships for vulnerable children, youth and families* (pp. 222–230). Alexandria, VA: Council on Social Work Education, Inc.

Hooper-Briar, K. & Lawson, H. A. (Eds.). (1996). *Expanding partnerships for vulnerable children, youth and families.* Alexandria, VA: Council on Social Work Education, Inc.

Lee, J. A. B. & Swenson, C. R. (1994). The concept of mutual aid. In A. Gitterman & L. Shulman (Eds.), *Mutual aid groups, vulnerable populations, and the life cycle* (2nd ed.), (pp. 413–430). New York: Columbia University Press.

Papell, C. P. & Rothman, B. (1966). Social group work models: Possession and heritage. *Journal of Education for Social Work, 2*(2), 66–77.

Roberts, R. N., Rule, S. & Innocenti, M. S. (1998). *Strengthening the family–professional partnerships in services for young children.* Baltimore, MD: Paul H. Brookes.

Shulman, L. (1992). *The skills of helping: Individuals, families and groups* (3rd ed.). Itasca, IL: F. E. Peacock Publishers, Inc.

Shulman, L. (1994). Group work method. In A. Gitterman & L. Shulman (Eds.), *Mutual aid groups, vulnerable populations, and the life cycle* (2nd ed.), (pp. 29–58). New York: Columbia University Press.

Shulman, L. and Gitterman, G. (1994) The life model, mutual aid, oppression, and the mediating function. In A. Gitterman & L. Shulman (Eds.). *Mutual aid groups, vulnerable populations, and the life cycle* (2nd ed.), (pp. 3–28). New York: Columbia University Press .

Zlotnik, J. L., McCroskey, J., Gradner, S., Gil de Gibaja, M., Taylor, H. P., George, J., Lind, F., Jordan-Marsh, M., Costa, V. B., & Taylor-Dinwiddie, S. (Project Collaborators). (1999). *Myths and opportunities: An examination of the impact of discipline-specific accreditation on interprofessional education.* Alexandria, VA: Council on Social Work Education.

3 The Genealogy of Group Work

The Missing Factor in Teaching Skill Today

George S. Getzel

Introduction: The Parable of the Young Group Worker

A young man is walking north on Lexington Avenue, under his arm a book, *Social Work with Groups, Third Edition*, when his path is crossed by an old fellow walking south with the same book under his arm. Curiosity piques the younger man and he asks his elder if he is a group worker. The old man quietly indicates that others would say so. Excitedly, the young man asks how he might become a group worker.

The old man shouts, "Practice!"

"Without a teacher?" he queries.

"Of course, you need a wise teacher."

"How shall I find such a teacher?"

"With great difficulty, because there are those who teach and don't know (confusing teaching with doing); and finally there are those who do and don't teach (because those who are ignorant and lack understanding stop them at the gate)."

Now the young man is confused and cries out, "Then how can I become a group worker?"

"Practice!" the old man replies, resuming his walk in the other direction.

* * *

For the whole of the 23 years of the existence of the Association for the Advancement of Social Work with Groups, there have been repeated expressions of concern about the demise of group work teaching and practice in schools of social work. The Association affords a platform for academics and practitioners to display the range of group work practice flourishing in different fields of practice. Journals have been initiated and many new textbooks written. Leaders of the Association have made valiant attempts at advocating for standards for social work practice with groups and persevered for their acceptance by the Council of Social Work Education (AASWG, 2002). Group work specific books on classroom teaching and field work support have been published in the last ten years (Kurland & Salmon, 1998; Wayne & Cohen, 2001). Despite these important and necessary developments, the status of education for group work in schools of social work and the field remains uncertain. In the current environment, the fragile threads of the transmission of group work concepts and skills from one generation of seasoned practitioners to the next is unraveling and disintegrating. In short, we are losing or have already lost the genealogy of group work practice.

This chapter has the following objectives:

- Examines the demise of group work teaching in the context of the attacks on professional education in universities and schools of social work in particular;
- Analyzes the university's preoccupation with technical rationality at the expense of teaching practice skills;
- Identifies the unique characteristics of education for practice skill;
- Defines the nature of the genealogy of practice with attention to humanistic values, intergenerational dynamics and the special influence of the *gift relationship*; and
- Makes recommendations to revivify and to reconstruct the genealogy of group work practice for future generations of practitioners.

Professional Schools in Crisis

No examination of the issues surrounding the demise of group work emphasis in social work education can avoid the larger contextual issue of the mounting antagonism within contemporary corporate universities to professional education and specifically the teaching of practice skills. For example, the newly inducted President of Columbia University halted the search for a dean for its school of journalism arguing that the faculty should diminish its attention to enhancing writing skills, and instead emphasize the role of journalism in society. Such a theoretical focus is deemed more in keeping with the mission of a first-ranked research oriented university (Arenson, 2002). Similarly, Harvard University's administration questioned the academic legitimacy of a studio art activity in their fine arts graduate program (Tomkins, 2002). I would argue a similar assault is occurring on the teaching of practice skills in schools of social work.

Anticipating this trend more than 15 years ago, Donald Schon (1987) in analyzing the crisis of confidence in professional education in disciplines as diverse architecture, music, urban planning, engineering, and psychotherapy wrote:

> In the varied topography of professional practice, there is a high, hard ground overlooking a swamp. On the high ground, manageable problems lend themselves to solution through the application of research-based theory and technique. In the swampy lowland, messy confusing problems defy technical solutions. The irony of this situation is that the problem

of the high ground tends to be relatively unimportant to individuals or society at large, however great their technical interest may be, while in the swamp lie the problems of greatest human concern. (p. 3)

Schon's analogy captures the disconnect that exists between social work faculty who are intellectually and emotionally wedded to theory-building research and its applicability to solving problems through technical rationality, and in contrast, the advocates of enhancing skill, the guardians of the flame of practice, see themselves as closer to the human condition and to the necessity for reflective, proximate, and artistic approaches to address the important problems facing people.

Schools of social work are facing a crisis from within and without as illustrated by their ambivalent attitudes toward teaching group work. Although students value field internships that allow them to do group work, they must struggle to get them and concurrent group work courses. Many faculty teaching group work are relegated to a lower academic status than others among the teaching professorate. In other practice contexts, social workers deem this as a condition of oppression. By the way, adjuncts in the schools of social work, yet a lower caste of the professorate, may be sought out to teach group work.

Limits of Technical Rationality

The renewal of teaching practice skills and by inclusion group work is *not* an argument against technical rationality and academic research, but a call for balance and equity of emphasis. Technical rationality opens new directions for human welfare. Pasteur's Germ Theory pointed the way to life-saving public health programs and the Laws of Thermodynamic Theory gave us steam-driven locomotives and electric generators. The prevailing hierarchy in universities gives the most esteem and rewards to the basic sciences, followed by the applied sciences and on the lowest rung, the technical skills of day-to-day practice.

Schon (1987) indicated the technical skills of everyday life involve "zones of interdeterminacy" that are characterized by uncertainty, uniqueness, and value conflicts (pp. 6–7). Uncertainty means that concepts or theories fall short or may not readily fit the problem configuration that faces the practitioner. Tough problems typically entail value conflicts: for example, do you stop group members from openly discussing their anger and ideas of physical retribution towards a group member who has relapsed into drug abuse or do you protect the scapegoated member by suggesting he leave the group? Social workers routinely assist people with these kind of knotty problems that do not have foolproof remedies grounded in technical rationality; they depend on an array of partial approaches and half-way solutions that must be adjusted to the changing circumstances, perceptions, and images embedded in the practice context. Group workers use artistic solutions to address uncertainty, uniqueness, and value dilemmas endemic to human existence. The classroom professorate teaches concepts and the general nature of practice, but the ability to know how to act with people occurs in the field. Group work in the field assists in the exploration of *knowing-in-action* and *reflecting-in-action* (Schon, 1987).

Allow me the use of a few non-group work examples of *knowing* and *reflecting-in action*. My son, a mechanical engineer, told me of a beloved professor he had who has spent his free time working out the physics of throwing a football; he identified the aerodynamic requirements for a football to pass from one point in space to another. Despite the brilliance of his theoretical calculations, this professor would not expect a young quarterback to successfully throw a football in a stadium during a windy Saturday afternoon in October on his theory alone. The football player must be coached and be given latitude to practice and to test out different techniques. The unity of intellectual, emotional, motor, and autonomic responses necessary to integrate football-throwing skills is *knowledge-in-action*.

In the same way, ordinary New Yorkers crowded together on subway platforms have developed the tacit *knowledge-in-action* to negotiate revolving gates one person at a time. This tacit knowledge is integrated into the smooth movement of people passing through the revolving gate in magical succession. *Reflecting-in-action* for subway riders is demonstrated by their wise decisions to avoid a crowded subway train and wait for the next one that is likely to be less crowded with more empty seats.

Experienced group workers have skills in the form of *knowing-in-action* that is revealed in their deft and intelligent actions with the people they serve. These skills occur in smooth, seemingly effortless actions with clients. By observing our actions during periods of high performance, we begin to make the tacit elements of actions and insights more explicit; we learn that there are patterns to our actions, value priorities and significant assumptions in our skillful actions.

The teacher of group work uses her gifts to create a culture of *reflection-in-action* with students using practice situations at hand. The task of the good educator is to explain the *artistry* in practice by assisting the student to develop useful *constructions* which "attempt to put into explicit, symbolic form of kind of intelligence that begins by being tacit and spontaneous" (Schon, 1987, p. 25).

The teaching/learning moment is found in the surprises that pop up during routine, tacit actions. These moments challenge intellectual, emotional, motor, and autonomic centers of response, not unlike a personal crisis. The teacher and learner are impelled to question implicit assumptions, to revise strategies to reframe problem definitions and to experiment with new actions. For the group work in the field, the teaching/learning moment may occur after a student has a particularly harrowing interview with an enraged adolescent mother in a parenting group. It may also happen when the veteran group worker notices that a student's written records never include a description of a member in the group, and the student's faces reddens when this is mentioned to him.

The rewards of group work education are fueled by these teaching moments and are themselves the stuff for *reflecting-in-action*. The practice within the group is the ultimate source of *knowledge-in-action* and the development of practice skills. Students are the legatees of enhanced practice skills.

Elements of Teaching

Teaching group work concepts and skills is *a humanizing endeavor* and an *intergenerational transfer* from a seasoned professional to a student in the form of a *gift* consisting of focused, shared *reflection-in-action* that enhances the student's skills and, in turn, is received as a *gift* by the group members she serves. Allow me to elaborate on three elements of this preliminary definition:

A Humanizing Endeavor

Group work education is first and foremost a humanizing endeavor to overcome the suffering and pain of members by reaching coherence between thought, feelings, and actions through the group process. The group work student quickly sees much human suffering and pain in the lives of people who form her group. With empathetic engagement of group members, the student resonates with the suffering she confronts. The student experiences helplessness, guilt, revulsion, confusion, unworthiness, and fear at different moments. The group work teacher, unlike the student, has more historical, social, and intentional understandings of the problems group workers face day-in and day-out. It is the group work educator's explication of the specific historical context of practice that turns insurmountable obstacles into pieces of a puzzle of yet larger processes that preceded the student's appearance. The group worker opens the student to the social context in which all problems are embedded and the cast of people who themselves are sources for solutions and mutual aid to supplement the student's puny efforts. Finally, the group work educator has experienced the human potential or intentionality hidden within oppressed and ill people. Intentionality is the human capacity to imagine a future. The educator demonstrates to the student the capacity of identifying the inchoate aspirations of people and of supporting group members' efforts to grasp a better future.

An Intergenerational Transfer

An overlooked or undervalued aspect of group work education is the underlying historical process of transferring practice artistry from one generation to another. It is not the literal reproduction of some sanctified rituals, but the evolution of practice skill responding to changing conditions building on the foundation of previous generations of practitioners who reflected on their actions and found ways of sharing their practice wisdom. If group work practice was wholly based on technical rationality, the need for the intergenerational transfer of skill would be irrelevant because there would be standard tools to address all predictable circumstances.

The artistry of practice passing to a younger generation consists of three elements: (1) the *transmission* of tacit and explicit references to certain practice approaches; (2) the *transformation* of those references that correspond to talents of the younger practitioner and current conditions; and (3) the *transference* in the form of an incorporated representation of the teacher into the active consciousness of the student.

The intergenerational character of practice artistry provides important instrumental benefits to group work education. A deeper understanding of the genealogy of practice skill and wisdom has instrumental and emotional value to the student and the teacher. The transmission of tacit and explicit references by the teacher provides a universe of references for the student that may be used in her current practice situation. The dialogue between student and teacher transforms those references for ready use in the here-and-now. Finally, the *voice* of the teacher is transferred to the student as she approaches new challenges in the field. The teacher becomes an *internal guide* for the students, particularly in challenging moments. It is not unusual for a student to say to a teacher, "When group members said. . . I heard your voice saying. . ."

All students should know the geological foundation of their skill. The example of a friend of mine may be useful; he grew up in West Virginia in a very dysfunctional family. An island of beauty in his life occurred during hours spent with his piano teacher who was a refugee from Nazi Germany. After playing a Chopin nocturne particularly well, he heard his teacher speak about playing the same music for her teacher, 40 years earlier. She then described a succession of teachers that went back to Beethoven. The young man never forgot that moment. In the same way, Jessica Getzel, a group worker and teacher I know, can say her genealogy of practice consists of Selma Stevens her field instructor of 30 years ago, who was taught by Catherine Papell, and in turn by Helen Philips, Grace Coyle, Eduoard Lindemann, John Dewey and Jane Addams.

A gift

The intergenerational transfer of the artistry of group work skill is a gift. Lewis Hyde (1979) in his seminal work, *The Gift: Imagination and the Erotic Life of Property*, writes that:

> a work of art is a gift, not a commodity. Or to state the modern case with more precision, that works of art exist simultaneously in two "econo-mies," as market economy and gift economy. Only one of these is

essential, however: a work of art can survive without a market, but if there is no gift there is no art. (p. xi)

We receive a gift not on the basis of our own effort; it cannot be bought or be acquired by our own strenuous efforts. We describe a special talent as a gift that has been conferred on us without our request. A talent is received as a gift and may be perfected by effort. Artistic inspiration comes as a gift to an artist who through her artistic production transfers the gift to an appreciative audience.

The worth of a gift is found in its continuous donation. Good stories and songs are wonderfully powerful gifts. A gift has psychic, intellectual, mythic, moral, aesthetic, and spiritual qualities that bear special attention. In group work education the exchange starts with the *gift* of working with people becoming a *gift* to teach a student, which is shared as a *gift* with group members who may translate the *gift* into acts of generosity and kindness to each other. Group work education continues to exist because of the non-remunerative rewards—psychic, intellectual, mythic, moral, aesthetic, and spiritual—that its generates and spreads. Therefore, schools of social work have a special obligation to maintain the conditions for this gift relationship to continue and thrive.

Turbulence to the Field

This is a very interesting time to be a group worker and a professional social worker. Recent developments in the economic, political, and social realms have left the social work profession in crisis as well. This crisis can be seen in our profession's inability to provide a coherent and unified response to the attacks being made against the human being through the decimation of health, education, and other social programs.

We are being told that the wave of the future is managed care, privatization, and syndicalization of all human and health services, as if this is a "natural" process, akin to earthquakes and monsoons, not subject to human action. Our professional associations give weak voice to this degradation of human services, with memberships more concerned with the questions of reimbursement for mental health services, acceptance by managed care cartels, and entrance into institutes for advanced psychotherapy. (The psychotherapy institute has become the latter day equivalent of Holy Orders in the Middle Ages.)

The work environment for social workers in many cases is becoming indistinguishable from that of the corporate world. Loyalty to the company, first and foremost; any signs of disobedience ("bad attitude") result in scrutiny from a supervisor and being escorted from your desk by a guard five minutes after being discharged. It is not so unusual to hear administrators ponder out loud, "Can we really afford these social workers? Might we substitute someone else at less cost and less trouble?"

The dehumanization of the social service workplace has reached alarming proportions in many instances, in both public and private agencies. The value conflicts and ethical binds of everyday work are daunting and provide fertile ground for the de-personalization, the de-professionalization, and the bureaucratization of the workplace—in which the human being becomes a means to an end.

As the situation worsens, group workers will find themselves increasingly in morally and spiritually compromised positions. For example, some large mental health agencies are asking group workers to process large numbers of people through groups in a perfunctory manner to increase censuses so as to fatten revenues. Such sham large-scale group programs weaken the collective strengths of already oppressed consumers and effectively deny them access to the healing power intrinsic to small group experiences. Many group workers already find themselves experiencing a fragmentation between what they personally believe and what they are asked to do in their professional lives. All these developments speak to a need for a courageous brand of group work practice that does not capitulate to anti-humanist practices as a standard of practice artistry. The group work educator in class and the field with her students must identify these deleterious conditions in social agencies, and fight to overcome the obstacles facing the poor and the oppressed. The school of social work must support group work practice as a powerful tool in the struggle to maintain values consonant with human dignity and welfare

Some Modest Proposals

We are familiar with the banal aphorism, "Those who don't do, teach." This aphorism does capture, however, an element of the current crisis in professional education for group work. I hear deans of schools of social work say that they cannot find group work teachers of practice among the current recipients of the social work doctorate. I hear students complain that they have teachers whose examples of practice are more than 30 years old or they have very intelligent young faculty teaching group work practice without ever having sustained practice outside of their internships in social work school. Practice teachers must move closer to the swamp-like conditions of actual group work practice in the field. If this does not happen, the marginalization of group work ideas and skill will deepen with graver repercussions. In this context, the following proposals are offered:

1. If the teaching practice skill inclusive of group work is the heart of social work education, there must be greater parity between those who are adept in group work in the field and the teaching professorate. Existing inequalities should be examined and remedied.
2. The actual or perceived high wall between field educators adept in group work and the teaching professorate should be strategically breached to

enhance useful practice research, to generate innovations in practice, and to upgrade group curriculum.

3. The designation of *national treasure* as used in Japan to honor great artists and artisans should be bestowed on stellar group workers in the field. These *national treasures* should have meaningful and organic connections to schools of social work.

4. The teaching professorate conducting practice classes in group work should carry meaningful group work assignments simultaneously with teaching.

5. More group workers adept in the method in the field should teach group work practice courses to keep classes lively and current.

6. Group work students should have a clear understanding of the genealogy of their practice and be encouraged to become teachers as they mature as practitioners.

7. Reflection-in-action should be strengthened through the establishment of *group work practice laboratories* to demonstrate group work in vivo; academic group work courses should be taught in the field; and *conservatories of group work practice in the field* should be established, just as we have nature conservatories to protect endangered species of plants and animals.

Conclusion

If there is anything worthwhile in this chapter, it is due to those who were part of my practice genealogy. I thank all my teachers living and dead for their wisdom, kindness and strength. Let us celebrate this legacy today and everyday.

References

Arenson, K. (2002). Columbia University, rethinking journalism school's mission, suspends search for new dean. *New York Times*, July 24, B. 7.

Association for the Advancement of Social Work with Groups. (2002). Standards for social work with group practice. Retrieved 9/15/02 from www.aaswg.org.

Hyde, L. (1979). *The gift: Imagination and the erotic life of property*. New York: Vintage Press.

Kurland, R. & Salmon, R. (1998). *Teaching a method course in social work with groups*. Washington DC: Council on Social Work Education.

Schon, D. A. (1987). *Educating the reflective practitioner*. New York: Jossey-Bass.

Tomkins, C. (2002). Can art be taught? *The New Yorker*, April 15, 44.

Wayne, J. & Cohen, C. S. (2001). *Group work education in the field*. Washington DC: Council on Social Work Education.

4 A Cross System Initiative Supporting Child Welfare Workforce Professionalization and Stabilization

A Task Group in Action[1]

Virginia Strand, Alma Carten, Diane Connolly, Sheldon R. Gelman, and Peter B. Vaughan

Introduction

Collaborations between schools of social work and human service organizations to meet common goals have a long tradition in social work. Schools of social work have worked in partnership with child welfare agencies around practice concerns, field instruction, policies affecting child welfare, and research for many years (Cohen & Austin, 1994; Hopkins, Mudrick, & Rudolph, 1999; Maluccio, 1997; Maluccio & Anderson, 2000; Tracy & Pine, 2000; Urwin & Haynes, 1998; Young, 1994). Successful collaborations have been developed between two or more human services agencies (Alverez & Cabbil, 2001; Gil de Gebaja, 2001; Henkin & Dee, 1998; Mulroy & Shay, 1997) and between universities and a number of community-based agencies (Powell, Dosser, Handron, McCammon, Temkin, & Kaufman, 2001). Social workers and attorneys (Maidenberg & Golick, 2001), social workers and physicians (Abramson & Mizrahi, 1996; Mizrahi & Abramson, 2000), social workers and other health care providers (Brown, Smith, Ewahlt, & Walker 1996; Christ & Somanti, 1999; Handron, Diamond, & Zlotnik, 2001; Howe, Hyer, Mellore, Lindeman, & Luptak, 2001; and Neufeld & Kniepmann, 2001) and social workers and school personnel (Caruso, 2000; Sessions, Fanolis, Corwin, & Miller, 2001) have also entered into joint endeavors. The need for continuing collaboration in all these areas has been articulated by Bronstein (2003) who views both the severity of client problems and the sensitivity to psychosocial aspects of education and health care as driving future collaborations.

1 We would like to acknowledge the contribution of Eileen Pentel and Adeyinka Adenira in the presentation of this paper in an earlier form at the 2002 Association of Social Work with Groups Symposium.

Collaborations can be understood as a special form of task groups. The goal of a task group is to bring about change outside the group, in the social, or in the case, the professional environment. The emphasis in task groups is on accomplishing a purpose, developing policies, a product or a plan, and as a means of participating in decision-making. Task groups may also emerge in order to evaluate a social policy or practice. Therapeutic groups, by contrast, are focused on bringing about change in the individual (Fatout & Rose, 1995). This chapter describes the development of large, multi-university collaboration with a public child welfare agency that was established in order to foster professionalization and stabilization of the child welfare workforce.

The phases of the development of the collaboration parallel those described for task groups. Fatout and Rose (1995) have identified four phases in the development of task groups: formative, beginning, middle, and end. The beginning stage is further divided into two sub-stages: one of orientation, in which members get to know one another and are oriented to the common purpose, and a second identified as "initial engagement" (Fatout & Rose, 1995, p. 59). In describing team development, another type of task group, Levi (2001) identifies five phases: Forming, Storming, Norming, Performing, and Adjourning. McGrath (1994) in writing about project groups, identifies parallel phases of group development. He labels these: inception, problem-solving, conflict resolution, and execution. Graham and Barter (1999) identify four phases which they believe to be specific to collaboration: problem-solving, setting the direction, implementation of a plan, and structuring the on-going collaboration

All four frameworks have similar themes. In the initial phase a task group must be planned, members need to affiliate and to articulate and agree on goals. Subsequently, there is typically a period of tension or conflict, often surrounding leadership conflicts, tensions between leaders and members, and participants' need to meet both individual and group goals (Fatout & Rose, 1995). There may be confusion around roles and project requirement (Levi, 2001). In functioning task groups, conflict is resolved and the group becomes cohesive, establishes norms, and reaffirms the group's purpose. The group is then poised to enter the working phase, which is often the longest stage.

Most task groups engage in evaluation, either as an on-going quality assurance measure or as part of a termination phase. Unlike research designed to advance practice knowledge, the purpose of task force evaluation includes "determining, evaluating and specifying the actions of the tasks force members as well as . . . others" (Fatout & Rose, 1995, p. 145). Some emphasize the need for evaluation of the impact of the task group's function on the external environment. Mulroy and Shay (1997), from their work with collaborations, believe that successful evaluation of a collaboration involves sustained observations of outcomes in the field, and usually combine both qualitative and quantitative methods (Mulroy & Shay, 1997).

This chapter describes a cross system initiative supporting child welfare workforce professionalization and stabilization which is an example of the interprofessionalism group approach described by Nina Aronoff and Darlyne Bailey in this volume. The initiative, the New York City Social Work Education Consortium, was developed to address shared concerns between the schools of social work and the public child welfare agency in New York City. Common themes exist in the description of collaborative efforts. In general, these include the presence of a shared problem to be addressed, the joint development of goals, shared decision-making in setting priorities, involvement of agency or organizational representatives who have the authority and influence to commit resources, the perception of mutually beneficial outcomes from any activities that the collaboration undertakes, and the ability to establish on-going structures that sustain the work of the collaboration (Daka-Muhwanda, Thornburg, Filbert, & Klein, 1995; Graham & Barter, 1999; Kagan, 1991; O'Looney, 1994; Subramanian, Siegel & Garcia, 1994; and Wimpfheimer, Bloom & Kramer, 1990).

The development of the consortium is described using the common themes in the frameworks described above: (1) Formation, (2) Group Tensions, (3) Development of Shared Norms, (4) Performance, and (5) Evaluation and Establishment of On-Going Structures. Each of the five phases is addressed in more detail below.

Phase One: Formation

In the first stage, the *problem* which initially mobilized formation of the New York City Social Work Education Consortium was the perceived need for further professionalization and stabilization of the child welfare work force on the part of important stakeholders. The motivation for the schools of social work and the public child welfare agency to join together in the New York City partnership can be examined from the perspective of these stakeholders. First, the motivation of the public child welfare agency—the Administration for Children's Services (ACS)—is considered, followed by consideration of the motivation of the seven schools of social work which joined the partnership.

In New York City, significant reforms had been made in the public child welfare system between 1996 and 2000. These reforms had resulted in a major change in the delivery of services, from a centralized system of operation to a neighborhood-based model. It had also resulted in an increased emphasis on accountability within the system, in developing more effective management and supervisory structures, in the infusion of MSW level staff in supervisory and advanced practice positions, and in solidifying best practice approaches. A concern about the turnover of staff and the quality of direct practice in New York City continued to be an issue of concern however, motivating the city to seek to increase the number of MSW level staff while continuing to emphasize in-service training for staff. The public child welfare agency initiated a scholarship program for staff interested in pursuing their MSW in 1997 and roughly 100 new staff a year were being supported through the scholarship program by the time the consortium was formed in 2000.

Thus, the city had committed substantial funds to graduate social work education for child welfare staff. From the perspective of the child welfare agency, its commitment to graduate social work education reflected a concern with upgrading and solidifying gains in the development of a professional practice environment. It was important for ACS that their employees learn how to integrate the theoretical and knowledge base of social work to the practice dilemmas faced daily by staff in order to ensure that the best interests of the children and families were being met. In addition, ACS employees tend to be older, with much experience, and ACS wanted to be sure that their learning needs were being met. ACS was motivated, therefore, to facilitate a process which would assure that the schools of social work were cognitive of the specific educational needs of staff and conversant with the goals of the ACS reform plan, specifically the move to community-based practice and the emphasis on parents as partners.

Additionally, from the perspective of ACS staff, the growth of the scholarship program presented many practical challenges, among them the need to relate to seven schools of social work, to seven sets of entrance criteria, seven sets of procedures for establishing field placements, and seven different protocols for advising and monitoring students in their field placements. The agency was faced with ensuring that the educational requirements of all of the schools of social work were met. It found, however, that at times the schools did not understand the operational aspects of ACS and could not always adequately assess field placements. More coordination would ensure that the needs of the school, the student, and the agency would be better met.

The motivation on the part of the schools to collaborate was partially driven by the increasing enrollment of scholarship-supported staff. However, as the numbers of staff from ACS enrolled in the MSW programs grew, faculty increasingly worked with these students in their classrooms, and as advisees, and became more invested in assuring a high quality educational experience for the public child welfare student. They also became interested in ways to work with ACS to help the child welfare agency retain MSW-level staff after graduation. Directors of field departments at the schools became more active in assuring that ACS staff matriculating into the MSW programs had an optimal experience in field placement, particularly since many were only required to take one year of field placement. Many students remained within ACS for work-study placements, making the development of and on-going monitoring of educational experiences a major quality assurance issue. Thus from the point of view of the ACS partner there were a variety of reasons to pursue this initiative.

The second partner, the New York City schools of social work, had an inconsistent history of working together as a group, and an even more erratic pattern of working collaboratively with the New York City public child welfare agency. Thus, before entering into a collective interface with the public child welfare agency, a major issue involved bringing the seven schools of social work together to explore whether or not a common agenda existed amongst them. This process was facilitated by the deans of the seven schools of social work in New York City, who supported the establishment of a common agenda around which to work with ACS. Of note is the fact that even within a such a collaborative effort there are even in groups having similar purposes differences that need to be resolved in the service of the common goals.

As the deans of the schools and ACS executive leadership moved forward, the commitment to collaboration was evident in two specific events: in the commitment of resources for a NYC coordinator, who could staff meetings and provide on-going administrative support, and in the establishment of a Steering Committee. The Steering Committee consisted of representatives from the seven schools of social work and seven to eight representatives from ACS. Both of these structures were in place by the summer of 2001.

Phase Two: Group Tensions

The second phase of collaboration—setting a direction—is characterized by activity aimed at identifying outcomes that the collaboration wants to achieve, by strategic planning, and by the specific identification of common values from which to operate. Struggles over power and control are typical in this phase and in struggles over leadership in particular (Powell et al., 1999). Tensions within the New York City Social Work Education Consortium became more apparent as the collaborative moved into this phase. Differences in perspective and misunderstandings characterized some of the interaction among members, stemming in part from tensions between the interests of social work education and the interests of the agency.

As noted above, an important step for the schools was the development of a sense of common ground among the seven schools of social work. Therefore, the schools convened a forum of deans, faculty, and directors of field departments to identify common concerns and prioritize issues. This effort was motivated by the need on the part of the schools to obtain faculty "buy-in" before approaching the public child welfare agency, as well as by a desire to take advantage of a funding opportunity. The results of this forum included suggestions for a number of activities which were then presented to ACS for consideration. This was, unfortunately, perceived initially by ACS as unilateral decision-making about the direction of the consortium on the part of the schools of social work, which exemplifies one of the tensions that can arise in a collaborative group when subgroups meet together to clarify their agenda.

ACS, for its part, had been involved in a massive reform effort for four years when the consortium idea surfaced in the late summer of 2000. Thus ACS had a clearer agenda. ACS professionals felt that the MSW curricula of the various schools were not supportive of, or always relevant to, child welfare practice. They believed that the schools were not sufficiently conversant with the reform plan and with the actual changes that ACS was implementing in frontline practice that, indeed, required and used social work skills. These changes included the practice of Family Team Conferencing in child protection as well as other programs, and the emphasis on strength-based, family-focused, and child-centered interventions. ACS was understandably proud of its achievements regarding the move to neighborhood-based services and the emphasis on parents as partners, and it was concerned that these reforms, among others, were not reflected in classroom teaching. Some staff believed that the schools of social work were not doing their part to inform and inspire students to go into child welfare as a field of practice. Their goals relative to the activities of the consortium, therefore, focused more on how the schools might be influenced to learn more about the reforms in ACS.

Additionally, ACS was looking for assistance with in-service training as well as an improved MSW program. Much of the in-service training is geared for the non-MSW employee, which continues to be the more typical profile of the caseworker in the New York City child welfare system. Training provides preparation for a specific job and while the training, an important emphasis at ACS, incorporates many social work theories and practices, it remains prescriptive for particular job functions.

Educators at the schools of social work take a broader view than those with a training perspective. Graduate education attempts to help the student make the necessary connections between theory, practice, and the values of the profession, including but not limited to the values of client self-determination and the uniqueness of every individual. The educated professional is one who is able to keep the needs of the individual child and/or family foremost while appreciating the constraints and limitation of organizational practice, and is able to keep a perspective of the whole rather than only concentrating on one specific department or job.

This tension between the goals of professional education and the need for in-service training was an underlying dynamic during this phase. It was important for the schools to be able to articulate their mission as educators and differentiate this from in-service training. The public child welfare agency wanted to tap faculty resources for in-service training. Limited faculty resources allow schools of social work to do little more than focus on the graduate education program. However, the needs of the agency also needed to be respected. Instances where a school of social work can assist with in-service training exist when a school has developed an infrastructure, usually with outside funding, focused on child welfare practice. Three of the New York City schools had such a structure, and these schools were positioned to assist with the in-service training needs of non-MSW staff. Therefore, the common ground for the consortium activities became the focus on pro-fessionalization of the work force through graduate education, and continuing education or on-going professional development opportunities.

Another tension was articulated by ACS-sponsored students. Field placements and course work often supported an administration concentration in the MSW program. However, most of the ACS scholarship students were enrolled in direct practice or clinical concentrations, and there was some sense that they were not always able to use what was learned in the classroom in their field placement. Additionally, complaints were being voiced that what students were learning in the classroom was not always supported by supervisors. This issue was also beginning to be articulated as a concern by graduates returning to work full time at ACS after graduation. Here again the issues of all stakeholders involvement came to the fore. Their issues became an issue that all parties were concerned about and where a need to take action was felt.

One other concern of ACS was that with the tremendous commitment in money and staff time to support staff in MSW programs, ACS program operations suffered from a depletion in staff. The agency wanted to have the consortium's assistance in exploring innovative ways to balance the educational requirements of the schools, the students' individual learning needs, and the needs of program operations. The schools as well as ACS had a shared commitment to addressing this issue.

As these issues surfaced, it became clear that an important step for the consortium would be the establishment of a forum to bring together a wider representation of agency staff and social work educators. This is consistent with an important development for most collaborations, that activities be linked at both the managerial and operations level (Mulroy & Shay, 1997). In engaging wider representation from both ACS and the school, the consortium was moving in that direction.

Phase Three: Development of Norms

This phase is characterized by stakeholders coming together to address issues, plan activities, and make decisions about the role and functions of members. As noted above, by the fall of 2001, the consortium had in place a coordinator and the structure of an Executive Steering Committee. The Steering Committee was in the process of planning a fall forum for faculty, administrators, and public agency management staff. As planning for the fall meeting took shape, it became clear that an activity which would strengthen acceptance and adherence to the consortium goals was advisable. It was decided to use part of the conference time to involve participants in the development of a values and principles statement, already drafted, that would guide the work of the consortium. In small work groups at the conference, participants addressed the questions: (1) "Does the Values and Principles Statement, as written, capture what you would like to see implemented in a collaborative effort between ACS and the schools of social work?" and (2) "Is there anything specific to New York City that you would want to recommend?" The work groups generated a significant number of suggestions. Pooling the responses produced a draft document for the Steering Committee to refine and then return to the wider group for acceptance, a process that was completed in 2002.

The development of norms was evident in the commitment to the mission statement, and to the development of faculty-led projects, with school and agency staff comprising the work groups for the projects. The process of coming to agreement on specific proposals positioned the consortium to move fully into the work phase of the task group process.

Phase Four: Performance

In the summer and fall of 2001, the Steering Committee of the consortium prioritized among a number of issues and identified four areas around which to collaborate. Each reflects a commitment to work on one of the issues identified in the beginning stage of the consortium development. These issues included the concern about further integration of the practice innovations at ACS into social work education programs, the concern about the quality of field placements, and the question of overall satisfaction of graduates with their professional education program. These were concretized into four proposals which were submitted for funding support. The projects are described in more detail below.

The first project pursued the establishment of a curriculum for field instructors and the delivery of this curriculum to a group of field supervisors. The goal of this project was to utilize community organizing techniques to better support and access/enhance neighborhood-based services in direct practice. The specific goals of the training program that was developed were (1) to help already-established field instructors refine their approaches to interpreting children's services within a neighborhood context for their students and (2) to provide the instructors with the specific organizing tools that could promote more effective professional–client partnership within a neighborhood context. These objectives were consistent with the movement within the child welfare system of organizing at the community level in order to mobilize an array of professional, lay, and religious organizations to share the responsibility in the delivery of services to those children and families coming to the attention of the child welfare system.

The purpose of the second project was to undertake an assessment of the experience of staff at the Administration for Children's Services who had completed the MSW program. The goals of the project were to:

1. Assess their experience in the different graduate school programs;
2. Inquire about how relevant their educational experiences were to their work;
3. Inquire about how they have been able to use their professional knowledge and skills in their work;
4. Inquire about how satisfied they are with their current job; and

5. Search for recommendations they have for improvement in the process at both the schools and ACS.

Preliminary results suggest that staff found their educational experiences gratifying regardless of the school they attended. If there was one area of concern it was that graduates felt that their new knowledge and skills were not utilized sufficiently once they were back in a full-time job, and that increased opportunities for on-going professional development would be beneficial.

The purpose of the third project was to examine the child welfare field placement experience for students in the MSW program through an evaluation of current field opportunities. Key study questions examined were:

1. Are current field placements sites consistent with standards established by the Council on Social Work Education (CSWE)?
2. Are field-work learning assignments congruent with the fieldwork programs of the various school of social work?
3. Are current fieldwork programs offered by the consortium schools preparing students for effective child welfare practice within the parameters of the ACS reform initiatives? and
4. How can fieldwork placements be improved and enhanced?

Findings suggest that current fieldwork placements are meeting CWSE standards and that learning assignments are congruent with field models of each consortium school. They also suggest that professional foundation course work offered by the consortium schools support broad-based skill development needed for child welfare practice. While students report being knowledgeable about contemporary issues of child welfare practice there was no strong evidence of structured standardized teaching of content related to strength-based practice or the requirements for documentation as a result of policy changes (e.g. the Adoption and Safe Families Act) in the field practica. The project also identified several areas about which more needs to be learned.

The fourth project was designed to provide the capacity for liaison, oversight, and coordination of NYC consortium activities and for long-term planning for future initiatives. Faculty and staff in this project helped develop the four project ideas that were eventually funded, worked with the deans to identify faculty members as project directors, and assumed responsibility for convening a workgroup of representatives from ACS, the voluntary agencies, and field departments at the consortium schools of social work for each project. This project also provided staffing for the Steering Committee, provided administrative support of the development and dissemination of the Values and Principles Statement, and for the sponsorship of meetings for all child welfare partners in November, 2001 and May, 2002.

Each of these projects extended over the 2001–2002 academic year and each has resulted in substantive findings that inform and continue to inform the consortium activities. Of interest is the finding in both projects two and three that of the three domains of interest explored in these studies—the classroom, the field experience, and the return to the agency—it is the third which returning staff point to as the area in which they would like to see the most attention devoted.

Phase Five: Evaluation and Establishment of On-Going Structures

The evaluation of the consortium's activities was informal and utilized the establishment of the consortium and original program objectives as outcome measures. The experience of implementing the four projects, working together on the Values and Principles Statement, and in convening two meetings of representatives of the entire partnership, led to the establishment of new relationships, the clarification of roles and functions, and a greater understanding of each others' institutions. It also resulted in important by-products that nurtured the on-going collaboration. For example, in the late summer of 2002, ACS requested additional assistance from the schools with the field placements of their MSW interns for the fall semester. In the past, while the assignment of placements was always undertaken in consultation with the schools, the consultation started when the process was well under way. Encouraged by the collaboration ACS requested that the schools and ACS jointly interview each of the prospective students at the very beginning of the placement process. This proved to be extremely helpful and efficient, resulting in the need for fewer re-placement of interns than in the past.

Another example of a positive outcome of the consortium was the assistance that faculty members and field placement staff gave ACS in evaluating the essays of the scholarship applicants. In the past, ACS assumed sole responsibility for this task, and it was helpful to have the consultation from faculty and field placement staff at the schools in this process. A third example is the identified need for on-going support of field instructors, resulting in the formation of a planning committee for a spring conference in the coming year.

One of the challenges at this phase is to sustain the initiatives made during the working phase of the consortium development; specifically, how to establish formal structures that will enable the consortium to carry its work forward. At this writing, the consortium has in place the

- MSW scholarship program;
- Monthly meetings of the Steering Committee for the consortium;
- A NYC Coordinator position;
- Promise of on-going funding;
- Continuing assistance from a state-wide university–agency collaboration;
- Regular, twice-yearly meetings of school and agency representatives;

- A statewide Advisory Council co-chaired by a dean and the commissioner of the state agency responsible for child welfare;
- Quarterly meetings of the deans of the schools of social work and the commissioner of the public agency.

Plans for the development of additional structures under consideration include the expansion of stakeholders to include the voluntary agencies, consumer groups (i.e. student representatives, and possible parent representatives) and representatives from the BSW programs. Additionally, discussions are underway for the establishment of an information and communication system.

Summary and Conclusion

The establishment of the consortium demonstrates the value of group process in developong and enhancing an on-going dialogue between staff at ACS and educators at the schools of social work. The process of creating a true collaboration in its focus on the establishment of common goals provided the opportunity to clear up a number of misconceptions on both sides. As the group worked through its tensions it was able to identify and implement specific, practical projects. As is true of successful collaborations there were gains for all stakeholders. The educational opportunities for ACS staff were strengthened, additional information on policy and the practice of social work in public child welfare became available to the schools of social work, and the potential for joint research was identified.

Staff at ACS will continue to have the opportunity for graduate education within the context of a more integrated, functional system that is more invested than ever in producing high quality practitioners and administrators. As the consortium continues to strengthen and grow the potential to achieve the goals in New York City of professionalization and stabilization of the work force in child welfare increases.

References

Abramson, J. S. & Mizrahi, T. (1996). When social workers and physicians collaborate: Positive and negative interdisciplinary experiences. *Social Work, 41*(3), 270–281.

Alvarez, A. R. & Cabbil, L. M. (2001). The MELD program: Promoting personal change and social justice through a year-long multicultural group experience. *Social Work with Groups, 24*(1), 3–20.

Bronstein, L. R. (2003). A model for interdisciplinary collaboration. *Social Work, 48*(3), 297–306.

Brown, C. V., Smith, M., Ewahlt, P. L., & Walker, D. D. (1996). Advancing social work practice in health care settings: A collaborative partnership for continuing education. *Health and Social Work, 21*(4), 267–276.

Caruso, N. (2000). Lessons learned in a city-school services partnership. *Social Work in Education, 22*(2), 108–116.

Christ, G. H. & Sormanti, M. (1999). Advancing social work practice in end-of-life care. *Social Work in Health Care, 30*(2), 81–99.

Cohen, B. J. & Austin, M. J. (1994). Organizational learning and change in a public child welfare agency. *Administration in Social Work, 18*(1), 1–19.

Daka-Mulwanda, V., Thornburg, K. R., Filbert, L., & Klein, T. (1995). Collaboration of services for children and families: A synthesis of recent research and recommendations. *Family Relations, 44*(2), 219–223.

Fatout, M. & Rose, S. R. (1995). *Task groups in the social services.* Thousand Oaks, CA: Sage Publications.

Gil de Gibaja, M. (2001). An exploratory study of administrative practice in collaboratives. *Administration in Social Work, 25*(2), 39–59.

Graham, J. R. & Barter, K. (1999). Collaboration: A social work practice method. *Families in Society, 80*(1), 6–12.

Handron, D., Diamond, J., & Zlotnik, J. L. (2001). Challenges of providing interdisciplinary mental health education. *Journal of Family Social Work, 5*(3), 49–62.

Henkin, A. & Dee, J. R. (1998). Collaboration in human services: Skills assessment for effective interpersonal communication. *Professional Development, 1*(1), 22–30.

Hopkins, K., Mudrick, N. R., & Rudolph, C. S. (1999). Impact of university/agency partnerships in child welfare on organizations, workers, and work activities. *Child Welfare, 78*(6), 749–773.

Howe, J. L., Hyer, K., Mellore, J., Lindeman, D., & Luptak, M. (2001). Educational approaches for preparing social work students for interdisciplinary teamwork on geriatric health care teams. *Social Work in Health Care, 32*(4), 19–42.

Kagan, S. I. (1991). *United we stand: Collaboration for child care and early education services.* New York: Teachers College Press.

Levi, D. (2001). *Group dynamics for teams.* Thousand Oaks, CA: Sage Publications.

Maidenberg, M. P. & Golick, T. (2001). Developing or enhancing interdisciplinary programs: A model for teaching collaboration. *Professional Development, 4*(2), 15–24.

Maluccio, A. N. (1997). Time for an ideological shift in child welfare: An essay review. *Social Service Review, 71*(1), 135–143.

Maluccio, A. N. & Anderson, G. R. (2000). Future challenges and opportunities in child welfare. *Child Welfare, 79*(1), 3–9.

McGrath, E. (1994). *Business psychology and organizational behavior.* Hillsdale, NJ: Lawrence Erlbaum.

Mizrahi, T. & Abramson, J. S. (2000). Collaboration between social workers and physicians: Perspectives on a shared case. *Social Work in Health Care, 31*(3), 1–24.

Mulroy, E. A. & Shay, S. (1997). Nonprofit organizations and innovation: A model of neighborhood-based collaboration to prevent child maltreatment. *Social Work, 42*(5), 515–524.

Neufeld, P. & Kniepmann, K. (2001) Gateway to wellness: An occupational therapy collaboration with the National Multiple Sclerosis Society. *Occupational Therapy in Health Care, 13*(3/4), 67–84.

O'Looney, J. (1994). Modeling collaboration and social service integration: A single state's experience with developmental and non-developmental models. *Administration in Social Work, 18*(1), 61–86.

Powell, J., Dosser, D., Handron, D., McCammon, S., Temkin, M. E., & Kaufman, M. (1999). Challenges of interdisciplinary collaboration: A faculty-consortium's initial attempts to model collaborative practice. *Journal of Community Practice, 6*(2), 27–47.

Sessions, P., Fanolis, V., Corwin, M., & Miller, J. (2001) Partners for success: A collaborative program between the Smith College School for Social Work and the Springfield, Massachusetts, public schools. *Smith College Studies in Social Work, 71*(2), 227–242.

Subramanian, K., Siegel, E. J., & Garcia, C. (1994). Case study of an agency-university research partnership between a school of social work and a medical center. *Journal of Social Service Research, 19*(3/4), 145–161.

Tracy, E. M. & Pine, B. A. (2000). Child welfare education and training: Future trends and influences. *Child Welfare, 79*(1), 93–113.

Urwin, C. A. & Haynes, D. T. (1998). A reflexive model for collaboration: Empowered partnerships through focus groups. *Administration in Social Work, 22*(2).

Wimpfheimer, R., Bloom, M., & Kramer, M. (1990). Inter-agency collaboration: Some working principles. *Administration in Social Work, 14*(4), 89–102.

Young, T. M. (1994). Collaboration of a public welfare agency and a social work: school: A clinical group supervision project. *Child Welfare, 73*(6), 659–661.

5 Mutual Empathy

A Means of Improving the Quality of Emergency Health Care Services Rendered to Marginalized, Addicted Individuals

Arielle Dylan

A human being is a part of the whole called by us universe, a part limited in time and space. He experiences himself, his thoughts and feelings, as something separated from the rest, a kind of optical delusion of his consciousness. This delusion is a kind of prison for us, restricting us to our personal desires and to affection for a few persons nearest to us. Our task must be to free ourselves from this prison by widening our circle of compassion to embrace all living creatures and the whole of nature in its beauty. (Einstein, 1949, p. 125)

Having worked for some time now as a frontline worker in a social-housing agency whose mandate is to house the "hardest to house," I have witnessed repeatedly the clash between our agency's efforts and the biases and misapprehensions of the larger community. From bad press and political strategizing aimed at closing this operation to emergency services that are wanting in professionalism, the tripartite message of disdain, disfavor, and fear is obvious. The rubric "hardest to house," when applied to the social topography of any metropolitan city, invariably comprises those who have severe mental health and/or addictions issues. Indeed it is not unreasonable to suggest that at any given time 90% of our client population consists of people wrestling with addictions issues: primarily crack cocaine and, to a lesser extent, alcohol and other drugs. The number of times we need to call upon emergency healthcare services, considering the high incidence of drug-related seizures, fights, accidents, assaults, and overdoses, naturally surpasses what would be needed with an unaddicted population.

On countless occasions I have observed emergency healthcare workers speaking callously and curtly with our clients in a manner that is not only disrespectful but stigmatizing, connoting a thinly veiled message of the addict as worthless entity. With a frequency too high to ascribe simply to drug-related behavioral problems, our clients return home from the hospital incompletely treated, often ripping intravenous tubing out of their arms because the sense of alienation, of otherness, they experience while in institutions of medical care is overwhelming.

This chapter identifies empathic failure as the principal reason for the unprofessional treatment of marginalized, low-income addicted persons by emergency healthcare workers. It is believed that through empathy, through "subjectifying" rather than objectifying the other (in this case the addicted patient) the problem of poor relations between emergency workers and disenfranchised patients presenting with addictions issues can be alleviated. There exists a wealth of literature pointing to the role empathy plays in effecting positive outcomes in the therapist–client relationship, and Miller and Rollnick (1991) emphasize the importance of empathy in work with addicted individuals. Having named empathic failure as the primary source of the problem, efforts to increase the empathic capacity of emergency healthcare workers would be a logical remedial step. A pragmatic empathy training program designed for emergency workers and suitable to the considerable budget and time constraints that influence hospital programming is outlined in this chapter. But first, empathy, the pivotal construct of this discussion, needs to be defined.

Empathy has been variously defined. According to the *Oxford English Dictionary*, empathy is the "power of projecting one's personality into (and so fully comprehending) the object of contemplation" (1989, p. 184). *The Merriam Webster's Collegiate Dictionary* defines empathy as the "action of understanding, being aware of, being sensitive to, and vicariously experiencing the feelings, thoughts, and experiences of another . . . without [their being] communicated in an objectively explicit manner" (online). Etymologically, empathy is rendered after the Greek word *empatheia* and from the German *Einfühlung*, meaning "in feeling" or, rephrased to be less syntactically awkward, "feeling into" (Hoad, 1993; Raines, 1990). Since its adoption into the English lexicon, the word empathy has come to have many variations and gradations of meaning (see Bohart & Greenberg, 1997). While empathy is generally held to mean understanding another's thoughts or feelings, nicely captured by the pedestrian metaphors to "walk in the other person's shoes" or to see a situation "through the other person' eyes," there are differences in the way this construct is conceptualized by different theorists (MacIsaac, 1997; Warner, 1996).

Usually empathy is seen as involving both an emotional resonance and a cognitive perspective-taking with another in some form of interaction (Jordan, 1997; Warner, 1997). Psychoanalytic theorists, such as Kohut, view empathy as part of psychoanalytic cure (Dan & Hill, 1996). Kohut defined empathy as "vicarious introspection," intimating that through examining our own experience we can learn how things might be for someone in a similar circumstance (1959). Kohut's fuller definition of empathy is "the capacity to think and feel oneself into the inner life of another person" (1977, p. 82). Margulies (1984) suggests beginning from a Keatsian condition of "negative capability" and then imaginatively projecting one's consciousness into that of another being. Unlike Kohut and Margulies, Rogers, a humanistic theorist, conceived of empathy as a state not a capacity, a state wherein it is possible to perceive the "internal frame of reference of another with accuracy, and with the emotional components and meanings which pertain thereto, as if one were the other person, but without ever losing the 'as if' condition" (1959, p. 210). To lose the "as if" stipulation is, according to Rogers, to move into a state of identification. While Kohut (1978) posits the "recognition of the self in the other" as the central dynamic in empathy, Rogers's richer conceptualization necessarily includes the obverse, that is, the other in the self (1959, p. 704). For Rogers, empathic understanding facilitates a kind of "intuneness," an awareness of interconnectedness, which is "in itself healing, confirming, growth-promoting" (Rogers, 1986, p. 130).

With Rogers's work as a springboard, the shift in emphasis from reciprocity to mutuality, pioneered by the postmodernist Stone Centre theorists, was a natural development in the on-going empathy dialectic. Among these theorists empathy evolved to be seen as an understanding context not only addressing the movement within the person (Rogers, 1980), but also the "movement between people (the relationship) along with the movement within each person" (Surrey, 1990, p. 3). Like Rogers, Stone Centre theorists believe that empathy is a necessary and sufficient condition for change: people "grow through active participation in an empathic process which enhances their sense of themselves as relational beings, able to join with others in relational connection" (Kaplan, 1990, p. 8). Empathy, for Stone Centre theorists, "affirms the importance of 'the between' and encourages relational awareness," as relationships are central to people's well-being, or expressed more poetically by Buber, "all real living is meeting" (Jordan, 1990, p. 12; Buber, 1958). Buber asserts that the sanctity of "the between" transforms meetings from I–It to I–Thou relationships, from monologic to dialogic interactions where the other becomes a subject rather than an object in one's thought processes (Buber, 1988; Snyder, 1994). Because empathy leads to an understanding of each other's subjective world, allowing for glimpses of fundamental human sameness despite apparent differences, it precipitates a direct movement from subject–object relating to subject–subject relating (Jordan, 1989). Empathy is essential to understanding that aspect of the self which is capable of we-ness, transcendence of the separate, disconnected self (Jordan, 1984). It makes the paradigmatic diametric positions of self versus other and egoism versus altruism indefensible as people come to understand that they are sustained by, develop in, and depend on relationships (Jordan, 1997).

For the purpose of this discussion, empathy will mean mutual empathy, defined in a way that is consonant with the view of Rogers and the Stone Centre theorists but with a variation. In mutual connection we can investigate our idiosyncrasies and individuality but also transcend our sense of a unique and separate self. Empathy of this order enables one to honor but not elevate individual gifts (Jordan, 1991). When empathy is mutual, not merely bi-directional, there is a distinct affirmation of the self and a paradoxical movement beyond the self, a sense of the self as belonging to a larger relational unit (Jordan, 1987). And it is here that I would suggest that empathy is more than an epistemic process: it is ontological, a state of being. The twentieth-century physicist David Bohm theorized that there are three major realms of existence: the explicate order, the implicate order, and a source-ground beyond both. The implicate order is a realm where all events, all things are enfolded in a wholeness, a unity that underlies the explicate world of separate things and events (Bohm, 1980). When engaged in mutual empathy, one gains access to the implicate order, and the sense of separateness (characteristic of the explicate order) gives way to intersubjectivity, where self in other and other in self are exquisitely experienced. The paradox of the joining process of mutual empathy is that one develops a more articulated, differentiated understanding of the other, and therefore responds more deftly, more specifi-cally, quite the opposite of what regressive merging would engender. Two people in mutual empathy are intimately connected with each other but never lose touch with their own individuality.

Major reviews of psychotherapy research by Orlinsky and Howard (1978), Bergin and Lambert (1978), Dent (1978), and Gurman (1977) have all pointed to the fact that relational qualities between client and therapist more greatly influence outcome than any particular clinical skills or techniques. And Orlinsky, Grawe, and Parks (1994) found empathy to be the key relational factor promoting strong therapeutic alliance and positive outcomes. While the emergency worker–marginalized addict dyad does not exactly constitute a therapeutic relationship, the centrality of empathy as conducive to appropriately rendered services obtains. The reasons for the effectiveness of empathic responding are manifold. Being empathically received has a healing impact in and of itself. As Rogers asserts, real change occurs with understanding and acceptance, when an individual is given the "permission to be" (1980, p. 64). Empathic reception of this sort is the strongest factor for change-making and affirmative human interactions, for it is through mutuality, through the experience of recognition, that we become more fully human (Kaplan, 1983; Warner, 1996).

Empathic understanding is particularly crucial when working with the client population being discussed. Without exception the people defined by the category "hardest to house" can be seen in one sense or another as victims. All of the tenants who live in the social housing site described above, have at some point disclosed to me personal narratives of childhood abuse and neglect, where they were subject to deprivation, cruel and unnecessary suffering, and oppression. Empathy on the part of hospital staff would be of great benefit to the disenfranchised, drug-addicted, obviously low-income client in need of emergency medical attention because "it neutralizes the client's sense of powerlessness" (Pinderhughes, 1979, p. 316). Warner (1996) argues that those who have not experienced empathic understanding in childhood possess a "fragile" sense of processing as adults, and therefore are especially in need of empathic relating. For such individuals, the ability to process experience is extremely hampered. Fragile processing can be said to typify the client population under discussion, as indicated by many signs, including unconventional behaviors, volatility, depression, and severe addictions issues. Not surprisingly then, when members of the "hardest to house" community leave their alternative lifestyle enclave and enter so sterile an institution as a hospital, they feel displaced, alienated. The experience would be made more bearable, less isolating, if they were met with empathic communion (Gibbons, Lichtenberg, & van Beusekom, 1994).

But there are barriers to mutual empathy, the primary barrier being that we are laboring with the concepts of an outdated worldview, the mechanistic worldview, and applying them to a reality that can no longer be understood in terms of these concepts. Western science, largely influenced by Cartesian thought and Newtonian physics, rests on the assumption of a primary reality composed of separate objects (Jordan, 1986, 1991; Wilber, 1995). A firmly embedded *weltanschauung* of discrete, separate entities is not amenable to an experience of joining, of meeting the other as self. Western psychological understandings have undermined the centrality of empathy by obfuscating the interdependence of human relatedness and promulgating instead the independence of the individual as the desired endpoint of human development, the hallmark of maturity (Jordan, 1989). And Darwinian theory, as applied to the social arena, has led to the development of a self-striving, competitive Western social ethos where the Baconian model of *mastery over* rather than the Platonic notion of *joining* holds sway (Jordan, 1991). Sadly, a quick inventory of significant historical events reveals we tend to dehumanize those over whom we have power. With an agentic ethic eclipsing the communal ethic, ground becomes fertile for "instrumental reason that objectifies everything around it, itself included," where humans become "the object of information, never the subject of communication" (Habermas, 1990, p. 341; Foucault, 1979, p. 200). As Habermas states, this kind of reason kills "off dialogical relationships [and] transforms subjects, who are monologically turned in upon themselves, into objects for one another, and only objects" (1990, p. 246). The precariously skewed agentic ethic of Western culture, the sanctity and freedom of the individual (typified by the super hero mythopoeia), poses serious obstacles to the apprehension and experience of mutual empathy.

With the notion of the separate self, comes the need for protective boundaries. The self needs protection not only from internal impulses but from external demands and otherness as well (Jordan, 1984). Additionally, the "image of the ideal human as powerful and capable . . . disenfranchises" others (Vanier, 1998, p. 45). Consider for a moment the scenario of the freshly scrubbed, neatly and professionally attired, knowledge-armed emergency hospital worker who far more approximates the image of the human ideal than the unkempt, unhygienic, often poorly educated, sometimes track-marked, drug-addicted individual. This visual dichotomy, striking as it is to the imagination, is shattering and isolating in reality. The marginalized person typically feels a profound sense of intimidation in the face of the distant, comparatively idealized other. The relatively empowered individual often shrinks from the presence of the marginalized other, fearing the differentness, wanting to maintain a distance so as not to be associated with the other's disenfranchised status. As Vanier (1998) asserts, we "are all frightened of those who are different, those who challenge our authority, our certitudes, and our value system" (p. 73). The primordial fear of the dissident, the symbolic subverter of conventional values, plays out as a classist dislike of poverty and difference. "Operating from the model of the separate self, fear and caution may be the first responses we notice that block the spontaneous expression of our innate generosity" and the ability to be empathic (Dass & Gorman, 1985, p. 23). The marginalized patient, particularly the kind who is demanding (as a bulwark against helplessness), whose reactions are unpredictable, may evoke a sense of vulnerability in the hospital professional; and the likely response, if the professional is operating from a paradigm of separate self, is a reluctance or inability to get involved (Dass & Gorman, 1985).

Even those who begin as empathic helpers can, through time and weariness, become "disaffected others," creating a psychological distance between themselves and the marginalized patient, limiting their similarities and underscoring their differences (Gibbons et al., 1994). The disaffected other begins to regard the disenfranchised patient with aversion, wanting to establish distance from the vulnerable individual for fear of being diminished by association. It is understandable that many hospital workers in an emergency ward who begin their careers with idealism and vigour become cynical and winded under the oppressive grind of poor working conditions, intense emotions, immense pressures, and a sense of futility in the face of crushing, irrevocable human trauma for which emergency treatment can do little. The emergency worker who is not worn out and possesses a comfortable sense of self could possibly respond empathically to the marginalized patient, while the worker without these qualities is liable to be overwhelmed in the presence of the unconventional other. As Jordan (1984) astutely observes, self boundaries that are either too rigid or excessively diffuse sacrifice the possibility of essential human connectedness, by projection on the one hand and narcissistic extension of the self on the other. The person who is interiorized with respect to self-knowledge has an awareness that is less narcissistic than it would otherwise be: the more introspective, the more detached from the self one can become (Wilber, 1995). And this place of detachment from the self proves a sound vantage point for mutual empathy.

Surely hospitals are designed with the intention of serving patients. In fact, deliberate rudeness is harmful and would be a contravention of the Declaration of Geneva and the Nightingale Pledge, respective credos of medical doctors and nurses (Davis, 1985). As well, the Hippocratic Oath, a guiding and standard-setting treatise of hospitals, dictates that the role of the allopathic doctor or assistant is to "help, or at least to do no harm" (from *The Epipedemics*, as quoted by Veatch, 1981, p. 22). Having identified emergency workers' empathic failure as a problem that precipitates inadequate and often curtailed treatment (because the patient decides to bolt rather than endure feeling stigmatized), the following question surfaces: What can be done in an emergency hospital ward setting to ensure that workers and disenfranchized, addicted patients can experience an empathic working relationship that safeguards individual rights, choices, and appropriate self-determination? This chapter proposes that a biweekly, four-seminar (four hours each) empathy training program would do much to eliminate the gulf between the two groups, facilitating more amicable, professional relations and, ultimately, improved service delivery. The proposal for the training program would be presented to hospital administrations, and its introduction to emergency ward staff would be predicated on the administrative imperative of providing respectful, thorough treatment to all patients, including marginalized, low-income, addicted individuals, for they, like anyone else, have a right to quality medical care.

There are many empathy training programs (see Barak, 1990; Corcoran, 1982; Evans et al., 1998; Herbek & Yammarino, 1990; and Pecukonis, 1990), but none deal specifically with improving the empathic response when working with highly marginalized individuals. Because of the unique client population to be assisted and the complex, postmodern conceptualization of empathy, it was deemed best to devise a new training program designed to promote a practitioner–patient experience of mutual empathy. The program involves nonbehavioural empathy training, a proven effective approach (see Corcoran, 1982), using instruction, education, meditation, and team building. The intention is to enhance empathic responding through means that foster longevity of the change, and this is thought to be best achieved through a profound experiential shift as opposed to an attitudinal change or the attainment of new empathic techniques. As Evans et al. (1998) suggest, "traditional methods in . . . teaching empathy" lack "endurance in the caregiving situation and, when perceived falsely as . . . empathy, maybe detrimental" to the practitioner–patient relationship (p. 460).

The first four-hour seminar in the series would begin by explaining to the group the purpose of the training program: that is, to increase empathic responding when working with marginalized, addicted individuals and, thereby, improve service delivery. Jordan's (1986) articulation of mutual empathy is succinct and would be proffered as our working definition: mutual empathy "occurs when two people relate to one another in a context of interest in the other, emotional availability and responsiveness, cognitive appreciation of the wholeness of the other; the intent is to understand" (p. 7). There would be an invitation to discuss the definition, to ask questions, offer input, or seek clarification. In fact all the seminars would be structured in a highly interactive way, creating a gestalt of interrelated inclusion, mirroring the relational ethic of mutual empathy. Next would be a presentation and analysis of issues that impact on socioeconomic status and sometimes eventuate in marginalization, for example, poverty, abuse, homelessness, racism, sexism, and classism.

Because the specified target population is addicted individuals, this first seminar would include an educational segment pertaining to addictions. The disease model and the biopsychosocial model would be presented as two paradigms that are not only helpful in understanding addictions issues but also useful in facilitating empathic responding. The disease model classifies addiction with other pathologies, such as allergies or diabetes, where there is a heritable component combined with external environmental factors (Margolis & Zweben, 1998). According to this model, loss of control over drug use, persistent use despite repeated negative outcomes, denial, and a tendency to relapse are the principal characteristics of addiction. Lewis (1991) enumerated four defining criteria of disease: an evident biological basis, a set of identifiable signs and symptoms, a predictable course and outcome, and a lack of deliberate causation. Lewis argues that drug addiction satisfies these criteria and that the grounds for considering drug addiction a disease are no less cogent than the grounds for considering other commonly accepted conditions as diseases. Most disease model theorists are of the opinion that it is a biochemical genetic substrate that forms the basis of drug addictions (Hesselbrock, 1995; Miller & Gold, 1991).The biopsychosocial model subsumes the disease model but also involves consideration of intrapsychic matters, learned or conditioned behaviors, and family and social influences that contribute to the initiation and persistence of drug abuse. The intent is to challenge, through use of these models, the common biases and stereotypes regarding addicted individuals. This first seminar would end with an experiential focusing visualization, wherein the participants will be led through a guided imagery scenario involving a professional interaction with a marginalized, addicted patient. This procedure is "deeper and more bodily concrete" than just talking about how one might feel (Gendlin & Olsen, 1970, p. 222). It "operates by supplying new possibilities for further consideration," and stimulating openness is consonant with the tenor of this seminar series (Kantor & Zimring, 1976, p. 257).

The focus of the second seminar is an investigation of holism versus fragmentation. Because Western thought is predominantly agentic, ego-centrism and individualism are more socially prevalent than sociocentrism and communalism. As Emerson states, human beings "live in succession, in division, in parts, in particles" but within people "is the . . . whole; the wise silence; the universal beauty, to which every part and particle is equally related" (1969, p. 95). Recent findings in quantum physics have corroborated what mystics and sages from all different traditions throughout the ages have taught: we are all interconnected. But Western thought has lagged behind quantum science, and the old mechanistic paradigm maintains preeminence, informing social understanding and influencing human interactions. Since research has indicated that "one tends to be more empathic when there are similarities between the experiences of the empathizer and the target person and in the personalities of the two," it is prudent to educate people with regard to interconnectedness (Corcoran , 1982, p. 91). People are not connected simply by personalities, interests, perspectives, experiences, and the funda-mental sameness of the human condition: people are connected by virtue of their existence. And once one becomes aware of this fact, the mutually empathic response is more natural, for the other and the self are inextricably entwined. As Capra and Steindl-Rast summarize, "in the new paradigm, the properties of the parts can be understood only from the dynamics of the whole . . . Ultimately, there are no parts at all. What we call a part is merely a pattern in an inseparable web of relationships" (1991, p. xii). To evoke a sense of interconnectedness, this seminar will end with a meditation (followed by a discussion) in which the participants are asked to visualize their hearts opening toward themselves, toward others in the room, toward the image of the disenfranchised, addicted patient and, lastly, to all humankind (Rinpoche, 1993).

As Lammert (1986) suggests, "Awareness facilitates contact—and in this case, the important contact is with the client and his or her experience" (p. 375). The third seminar will have awareness as its theme and will underscore the importance of self-awareness, and awareness of others, while bridging some of the main ideas from the first and second seminars. The helping relationship as a power relationship will be discussed. Participants will be asked to identify and examine their own biases and understand the dynamics of those biases; to consider their tolerances and intolerances for differences; to understand that feelings can be delicate and behaviors aberrant in any situation that involves a definite power differential; and to acknowledge the role of ineluctable forces that often shape the lives of marginalized people (Pinderhughes, 1979). Because "an empathic approach requires a capacity for reflection and self-awareness," these mental exercises that stimulate self-reflection and contextualization of self and other in tangible terms better enable one to empathize (Bennett, Legon, & Zilberfein, 1989). "Heightened awareness of self . . . results in a heightened ability to see, through one's senses, where a client is and a greater willingness to flow with the client" (Lammert, 1986, p. 375). The final segment of this seminar would be a repeat of the visualization exercise from the first seminar. Participants could observe any changes that have occurred over the month since the training program's commencement. A closing discussion would follow.

All three of the preceding seminars have focused on improving the relationship between the practitioner and the patient. The tack has been to deconstruct the notion of the separate self, and to substitute the concept of relational selves. If this process occurs on a sufficiently deep level, there exists the possibility of abandoning those self boundaries that are overweening and allowing the worker to "feel the client's feeling reverberate within [her] own being" (Raines, 1990, p. 4). While this fourth seminar will recapitulate the essential elements of the previous seminars, inviting group discussion and providing further elaboration of any points that remain unclear, it will also introduce a final tenet: namely, empathic workers need empathic support. It is true that the survival of the hospital institution today is contingent upon regulatory economic factors, often meaning increased pressure on workers and less time for self care. But empathic workers need a community of other empathic workers; "without this supportive base it is too easy for workers to become isolated and overwhelmed and to disidentify and project in an attempt to protect themselves from these feelings" (Gibbons et al., 1994, p. 221). The challenge of this seminar's discussion will be to develop creative but practicable methods for making time for empathic support among the staff team in an environment that is generally inhospitable to seemingly inexpedient matters. Certainly the seminar facilitator could present some options (e.g., incorporating extra time into shift changes and staff meetings expressly for empathic support, working on developing a strong team sensibility that regards a member's need for empathic support as a team need, etc.), but the ideas generated by the group would likely be more germane. This seminar would end with the same meditation used in the second session but this time the final focus of the meditation would be the interconnectedness of the staff team. A general discussion would follow.

Having felt distressed by repeatedly witnessing the unprofessional, sometimes abusive, behavior of emergency hospital workers toward disenfranchised, addicted individuals in need of emergency care, I found myself returning in my mind again and again to the situation, haunted by images, contemplating if not solutions at least improvements. A training program having mutual empathy as its theme seemed to be an approach that holds out the promise of more than a stopgap measure. If one can undergo a profound inward shift in understanding, so that one begins to think of and see and sense the other as deeply related to oneself, then disrespectful relations become untenable (except in moments when this knowing is obscured). A mutual empathy training program which utilizes sociological, scientific, and philosophical educational segments (pertaining to knowledge of the self and the specified target group), a pedagogical tautology and cross-referencing of sources, as well as exercises in experiential simulation could produce the desirable shift and end the crisis of perception.

Wisdom knows that behind the Many is the One. (Wilber, 1995, p. 327)

References

Barak, A. (1990). Counselor training in empathy by a game procedure. *Counselor Education and Supervision, 29*(3), 170–178.

Bennett, C. J., Legon, J., & Zilberfein, F. (1989). The significance of empathy in current hospital based practice. *Social Work in Health Care, 14*(2), 27–41.

Bergin, A. E. and Lambert, M. J. (1978). The evaluation of therapeutic outcomes. In S. L. Garfield & A. E. Bergin (Eds.), *Handbook of psychotherapy and behavior change: An empirical analysis* (pp. 139–190). New York: Wiley.

Bohart, A. C. & Greenberg, L. S. (Eds.) (1997). *Empathy reconsidered: New directions in psychotherapy.* Washington, DC: American Psychological Association.

Bohm, D. (1980). *Wholeness and the implicate order.* London: Routledge and Kegan Paul.

Buber, M. (1958). *I and Thou.* R. G. Smith (Trans.). New York: Charles Scribner's and Sons.

Buber, M. (1988). *The knowledge of man: A philosophy of the interhuman.* Atlantic Highlands, NJ: Humanities Press International.

Capra, F. & Steindl-Rast, D. (1991). *Belonging to the universe.* San Francisco: Harper.

Corcoran, Kevin J. (1982). Behavioral and nonbehavioral methods of developing two types of empathy: A comparative study. *Journal of Education for Social Work, 18*(3), 85–93.

Dan, C. & Hill, C. E. (1996). The current state of empathy research. *Journal of Counseling Psychology, 43*(3), 261–274.

Dass, R. & Gorman, P. (1985). *How can I help?: Stories and reflections on service.* New York: Alfred A. Knopf.

Davis, F. A. (Ed.). (1985). *Taber's cyclopedic medical dictionary.* Philadelphia: F. A. Davis Company.

Dent, J. K. (1978). *Exploring the psycho-social therapies through the personalities of effective therapists.* Rockville, MD: National Institute of Mental Health.

Einstein, A. (1949). *The world as I see it.* New York: Philosophical Library.

Emerson, R. W. (1969). *Selected prose and poetry.* Ed. by R. L. Cook. San Francisco: Rinehart Press.

Evans, G. W., Wilt, D. L., Alligood, M. R., & O'Neil, M. (1998). Empathy: A study of two types. *Issues in Mental Health Nursing, 19*(5), 453–461.

Foucault, M. (1979). *Discipline and punish.* New York: Vintage.

Gendlin, E. T. & Olsen, L. (1970). The use of imagery in experiential focusing. *Psychotherapy: Theory, Research and Practice, 7*(4), 221–223.

Gibbons, D., Lichtenberg, P., & van Beusekom, J. (1994). Working with victims: Being empathic helpers. *Clinical Social Work Journal, 22*(2), 211–222.

Gurman, A. S. (1977). The patient's perception of the therapeutic relationship. In A. S.Gurman & A. M. Razin (Eds.), *Effective psychotherapy: A handbook of research* (pp. 503–543). New York: Pergamon Press.

Habermas, J. (1990). *Philosophical discourse of modernity.* Cambridge, MA: MIT Press.

Herbek, T. & Yammarino, F. J. (1990). Empathy training for hospital staff nurses. *Group & Organization Studies, 15*(3), 279–295.

Hesselbrock, V. M. (1995). The genetic epidemiology of alcoholism. In H. Begleiter and B. Kissin (Eds.), *The genetics of alcoholism* (pp. 17–39). New York: Oxford University Press.

Hoad, T. F. (Ed.). (1993). *The concise Oxford dictionary of English etymology.* Oxford: Oxford University Press.

Jordan, J. V. (1984). *Empathy and self boundaries. Work in Progress 16.* Wellesley, MA: Stone Center for Developmental Services and Studies.

Jordan, J. V. (1986). *The meaning of mutuality. Work in Progress 23.* Wellesley, MA: Stone Center for Developmental Services and Studies.

Jordan, J. V. (1987). *Clarity in connection: Empathic knowing, desire and sexuality. Work in Progress 29.* Wellesley, MA: Stone Center for Developmental Services and Studies.

Jordan, J. V. (1989). *Relational development: Therapeutic implications of empathy and shame. Work in Progress 39.* Wellesley, MA: Stone Center for Developmental Services and Studies.

Jordan, J. V. (1990). *Relational development through empathy: Therapeutic applications. Work in Progress 40,* 11–14. Wellesley, MA: Stone Center for Developmental Services and Studies.

Jordan, J. V. (1991). *The movement of mutuality and power. Work in Progress 53.* Wellesley, MA: Stone Center for Developmental Services and Studies.

Jordan, J. V. (1997). Relational development through mutual empathy. In A. C. Bohart & L. S. Greenberg (Eds.), *Empathy reconsidered: New directions in psychotherapy* (pp. 343–352). Washington, DC: American Psychological Association.

Kantor, S. & Zimring, F. M. (1976). The effects of focusing on a problem. *Psychotherapy: Theory, Research and Practice, 13*(3), 255–258.

Kaplan, A. G. (1983). *Empathic communication in the psychotherapy relationship. Work in Progress 82-02* (pp. 12–16). Wellesley, MA: Stone Center for Developmental Services and Studies.

Kaplan, A. G. (1990). *Empathy and its vicissitudes. Work in Progress 40*, 6–10. Wellesley, MA: Stone Center for Developmental Services and Studies.

Kohut, H. (1959). Introspection, empathy, and psychoanalysis: An examination of the relationship between mode of observation and theory. *Journal of the American Psychoanalytic Tradition, 7*, 459–483.

Kohut, H. (1977). *The restoration of the self.* New York: International Universities Press.

Kohut, H. (1978). The psychoanalyst in the community of scholars. In P. Ornstein (Ed.), *The search for the self: Selected writings of Heinz Kohut, Vol. 2.* New York: International Universities Press.

Lammert, M. (1986). Experience as knowing: Utilizing therapist self-awareness. *Social Casework: The Journal of Contemporary Social Work, 67*(6), 369–376.

Lewis, D. C. (1991). Comparison of alcoholism and other medical diseases: An internist's view. *Psychiatric Annals, 21*, 256–265.

MacIsaac, D. (1997). Empathy: Heinz Kohut's contribution. In A. C. Bohart & L. Greenberg (Eds.), *Empathy reconsidered: New directions in psychotherapy* (pp. 245–264). Washington, DC: American Psychological Association.

Margolis, R. D. and Zweben, J. E. (1998). *Treating patients with alcohol and other drug problems: An integrated approach.* Washington, DC: American Psychological Association.

Margulies, A. (1984). Toward empathy: The uses of wonder. *American Journal of Psychiatry, 23*(1), 4–20.

Merriam Webster. (2002). *Merriam Webster's dictionary.* Available at: http://www.m-w.com/dictionary/empathy

Miller, N. S. and Gold, M. S. (1991). *Alcohol.* New York: Plenum Medical.

Miller, W. R. and Rollnick, S. (1991) *Motivational interviewing: Preparing people to change addictive behaviour.* New York: Guilford Press.

Orlinsky, D. and Howard, K. (1978). The relation of process to outcome in psychotherapy. In S. L. Garfield & A. E. Bergin (Eds.), *Handbook of psychotherapy and behavior change: An empirical analysis* (pp. 283–330). New York: Wiley.

Orlinsky, D. E., Grawe, K., and Parks, B. K. (1994). Process and outcome in psychotherapy. In A. E. Bergin & S. L. Garfield (Eds.), *Handbook of psychotherapy and behaviour change* (pp. 270–378). New York: John Wiley and Sons.

Oxford English Dictionary (1989). *The Oxford English dictionary, 2nd Edition*, Vol. 5. Oxford: Clarendon Press.

Pecukonis, E. V. (1990). A cognitive/affective empathy training program as a function of ego development in aggressive adolescent females. *Adolescence, 25*(97), 59–76.

Pinderhughes, E. B. (1979). Teaching empathy in cross-cultural social work. *Social Work: Journal of the National Association of Social Workers, 24*(4), 312–316.

Raines, J. C. (1990). Empathy in clinical social work. *Clinical Social Work Journal, 18*(1), 57–72.

Rinpoche, S. (1993). *The Tibetan book of living and dying.* New York: HarperCollins.

Rogers, C. R. (1959). A theory of therapy, personality and interpersonal relationship as developed in the client centered framework. In S. Koch (Ed.) *Psychology: A study of a science* (Volume 3, *Formulations of the person and the social context*) (pp. 184–256). New York: McGraw-Hill.

Rogers, C. R. (1980). *A way of being.* Boston: Houghton Mifflin.

Rogers, C. R. (1986). Rogers, Kohut and Erickson: A personal perspective on some similarities and differences. *Person-Centered Review, 1,* 125–140.

Snyder, M. (1994). The development of social intelligence in psychotherapy: Empathic and dialogic processes. *Journal of Humanistic Psychology, 34*(1), 84–108.

Surrey, J. L. (1990). *Empathy: Evolving theoretical perspectives. Work in Progress 40,* 1–5. Wellesley, MA: Stone Center for Developmental Services and Studies.

Vanier, J. (1998). *Becoming human.* Toronto: Anansi.

Veatch, R. M. (1981). *The theory of medical ethics.* New York: Basic Books.

Warner, M.S. (1996). How does empathy cure?: A theoretical consideration of empathy, processing and personal narrative. In R. Hutterer, G. Pawlowsky, P. F. Schmid, & R. Stipsits (Eds.), *Client centered and experiential psychotherapy* (pp. 127–143). New York: Peter Lang.

Warner, M. S. (1997). Does empathy cure? A theoretical consideration of empathy, processing, and personal narrative. In A. C. Bohart & L. S. Greenberg (Eds.), *Empathy reconsidered: New directions in psychotherapy* (pp. 125–140). Washington, DC: American Psychological Association.

Wilber, K. (1995). *Sex, ecology, spirituality: The spirit of evolution.* Boston: Shambhala.

6 Assessing Skills in Groupwork

A Program of Continuing Professional Development[1]

Mark Doel

Introduction

This chapter presents the findings of an action research project in a main-stream social services agency in Britain. The aims of the project are:

- To *develop a groupwork service* in a public social work agency;
- To *teach a model of groupwork practice* which is relevant to practitioners working with a wide variety of service user groups;
- To *evaluate the group members' experiences* of the groups;
- To *assess the practitioners' skills as groupworkers* in a systematic way;
- To link these assessments to the agency's formal system of *continuing professional development* (CPD) and career progression.

A brief background to the Groupwork Project is presented. However, the reader should refer to previous works for a detailed background to the project (Doel & Sawdon, 1995, 1999a, 1999b, 2002). This chapter focuses on the way in which social workers' groupwork skills are assessed as part of the agency's program of career progression and continuing professional development, and the diversity of groups and groupwork which the program encompasses.

This chapter explores a holistic approach to assessing groupwork practice, using a *signposted portfolio*, a research tool developed by the project. On the basis of analysis of 47 completed portfolios of groupwork practice, I explore the effectiveness of this system in helping groupworkers to present evidence of their groupwork skill and to become reflective groupworkers.

Finally, the Groupwork Project is considered in the context of the agency's program of continuing professional development.

·

1   With thanks and acknowledgements to Catherine Sawdon, my friend and partner in the Groupwork Project.

The Groupwork Project

The Context

The Groupwork Project began in response to a desire to develop a groupwork service for clients of a social work agency in the north of England. Initially, a training program in groupwork was offered as a short course for staff across the agency, whether qualified in social work or not. It proved attractive, not just because of the interest in groupwork, but also because it brought practitioners together from very different corners of the agency. Field workers, hospital workers, residential and day care staff working with all sectors (children, adults, elders) found this was one of very few courses which crossed the usual divides between the different sectors of the agency.

During the 1990s, a framework for post-qualifying training in social work became clearly established in England (CCETSW, 1992). Practitioners and agencies also became increasingly concerned to demonstrate that learning had taken place as a result of training, and that there were tangible benefits to clients (Sheldon & Chivers, 2000). Staff taking part in the program (whom we will call *learners*) were required to provide evidence of the outcome of their training. Post-qualifying programs developed structures for learners to provide this evidence and systems to assess the evidence. These systems needed to mesh with the wider post-qualifying structures developed by the British national regulatory body and to award credits which were transferable and which would accrue to a Post-Qualifying Award in Social Work (PQSW).

The project has the experience of nine cohorts of learners, making a total of 121 learners (an average of 13.4 learners per cohort). Of these, 57 (47%) were qualified social workers and 59 (49%) pre-qualified. In addition, two learners were qualified in a profession other than social work (teaching and nursing respectively), two were student social workers on placement in the agency, and one was a volunteer worker who was a service user co-working the group with a qualified social worker.

Fifty-three groups have been successfully launched as a result of the Groupwork Project, and an unknown number of additional groups have been established as *spin-offs* from the project. Forty-six (87%) of the groups in the project were facilitated by more than one worker; in other words, most of the learners were co-working a group. Co-working and co-learning were promoted first on the basis of the perceived benefits of co-working (Hodge, 1985) and later in response to the evidence from the project itself.

The Overall Project

Very briefly, the Groupwork Project consists of three elements:

1. *The Training Program*

The training program in groupwork skills comprises a series of workshops and consultations held in the agency's training department. There are six workshop days and three one-hour consultations spread over a period of six months. The consultations are held between the course tutors and each pair of learners in the program. The learners' supervisors (line managers) are also invited to the first consultation, which takes place before the workshops begin, in order to commit them to each learner's involvement. Learners are encouraged to make joint applications to the program (usually as a pair, occasionally more). The application pro-forma for the program requires pairs of learners to outline their ideas for a group, with an expectations that each pair will be co-leaders with their planned group.

The project has also enabled us to develop and test a groupwork practice model (not the focus of this chapter, and more details can be found in Doel & Sawdon, 1999b). This is a generic practice model, providing an umbrella under which a surprisingly wide variety of groupwork methods can be accommodated, from non-directive approaches to solution-focused practice (Sharry, 2001).

2. The Groups

The second element is the group itself, which each learner or pair of learners develops and facilitates in parallel with the training program. In this way, the practitioners practice the learning they derive from the training program, by recruiting for a group, leading or facilitating the group, evaluating it and, where appropriate, ending the group. The project has spawned a wide diversity of groups (see Figure 6.1).

3. The Assessment of the Groupworker's Abilities

The third element is the assessment of the learners' groupwork practice. Each learner is taught how to gather evidence of their groupwork and to compile it in a portfolio to be submitted to a panel for assessment. There is an additional (seventh) workshop day focusing specifically on portfolio work. Following the submission and grading of the portfolio, there is an individual *viva voce* for each learner, which enables him or her to elaborate on the material already presented in the portfolio. The External Assessor participates in the viva. Some learners are referred to do further work on certain aspects of their portfolio, usually because they need to present additional evidence or demonstrate wider reading. Once successful, those learners who are qualified social workers are awarded 60 post-qualifying credits (which is half of the 120 credits needed for the Post-Qualifying Award in Social Work); those who are not qualified in social work are awarded an agency certificate of recognition and their portfolios can count towards future educational achievement.

In addition to developing the professional practice of its practitioners, the project is enabling the agency to develop a whole range of new groupwork services for its clients. The quality and outcomes of the groupwork are closely scrutinized, by virtue of the assessment of the learner's practice. And the

Being in Care Group: A group for young people to discuss issues of living in residential care.

The Chestnuts: A group for about twelve older people with varying degrees of dementia who were socially isolated.

Girls Just Wanna Have Fun: A distinctly "not therapy" group for eight girls, aged 14 to 15 years old, looking at self-esteem, sex, drugs and enjoyable activity.

Home Carers' Groups: A series of groups to assist home carers in the agency to consider policy, procedure and practice, and to develop mutual support and understanding.

It Does Matter. (Group name changed by members from provisional name, *What Matters?*). A group for eight members focusing on mental health issues and stress management strategies.

Looking Good, Feeling Good: (Group name changed by members from *Mirror Image*). A group to promote self-confidence and self-esteem, and a greater understanding of anxiety and ways of coping. For nine women aged between 30 and 60 years, the group met once a week for nine two-hour sessions.

Memory Joggers: A group for older people with mild or moderate dementia; the groupwork service was developed to meet a deficit in provision, in order to provide group stimulation and help with memory.

Offending Behaviour Group: A group for seven young people, meeting twice weekly over ten weeks to look at victims, anger management, offending behaviour, thinking skills.

Parenting Group: A group from parents experiencing difficulties with the behaviour of their children.

School Group: A group for five girls and three boys aged 12 to 13 "in trouble more than most". The young people felt able to solve problems in this group jointly led by a teacher and a social work assistant.

TAG (Temporary Accommodation Group): A group for young people seeking accommodation and needing preparation for independent accommodation.

The Women's Group: This group brought together four women who had been sexually abused; it was planned as weekly for six weeks but actually ran for 30 sessions.

Women Forward Group: A group in a day training centre for women with learning difficulties. The group had a profound impact (for good), but provoked intense jealousies amongst other day care workers and the intended follow-up groups did not happen.

The Youngsters' Group: A group for six young people aged 8 to 12 years who had or were experiencing domestic violence.

Figure 6.1 Some Examples from the 53 Groups in the Groupwork Project

impact of the groupwork on the agency's clientele is documented in the portfolios, in which clients' names are suitably anonymised.

The Groupwork Project has shown that groupwork is possible in a mainstream social work agency, despite concerns that it has fallen off the social work map (Ward, 1998). The experience of the project has also brought to light much groupwork in the "penumbra" of the agency; groupwork which the agency hardly knows is taking place, often involving staff with relatively low status in the agency. Nevertheless, these groups in the agency's shadows are providing a regular and rewarding experience for many people. Finally, many learners in the project remark on the way their antennae for groupwork are sharpened by the program, so they become much more aware of their teams *as groups* and use their groupwork skills to enhance their teamwork. They develop "groupwork literacy" (Doel, 2006)

Partial and Holistic Approaches to Assessment of Groupwork Ability

The practice of professional staff in an agency needs regular assessment to ensure the quality of service in the agency. In terms of groupwork, group members need confidence that the standard of groupworkers has been properly assessed. At a very basic level this concerns the emotional and physical safety of group members.

It is equally important that we find ways of making assessments of practice which are fair, accurate and efficient. In addition, assessment systems should be *congruent* with learning; in other words, the assessment methods and processes should not hinder the learning and, if possible, they should accelerate it but not drive it. Assessment will involve the *evaluation* of the group and the groupwork, but its focus is on judgments made about the learner/groupworker's practice.

In England, the debate around the assessment of professional practice, groupwork or otherwise, has become polarized around proponents of partial approaches on the one hand and holistic approaches on the other. The former has tended to become identified with competencies (O'Hagan, 1996); the latter with the notion of reflective practice (Yelloly & Henkel, 1995). The former has a relatively strong grip on government bodies and agency managers; the latter has more proponents amongst practitioners and educators.

The argument that this is a false dichotomy has been made in greater detail elsewhere (Doel, Sawdon & Morrison, 2002, pp. 30–35). Suffice it to note here that one level of understanding is gained by partializing a complex activity into its different and separate parts, and another is acquired by viewing the whole activity in its context. The partial approach helps to acquire skills which improve performance. The contextual enables us to relate the groupwork practice to broader frameworks which reveal its many *meanings*. On the one hand groupworkers need to learn how to identify and employ different techniques at an interpersonal level within the group (partializing);

on the other hand, they should also have an understanding of wider social forces and the impact of discrimination on individual group members (contextualizing). To achieve success, many groups need the support of champions in agencies or communities, to ensure the group is adequately resourced and promoted. An individual group might flourish, but without an understanding of these contextual factors, as a groupwork *service* it is likely to flounder.

By reframing the notion of holism, we can see that a holistic approach embraces both the partial and the contextual. Groupwork is a complex activity and cannot be measured in a single dimension; skilled groupwork takes account of what is happening outside and around the group as well as what is happening within it. A holistic approach enables us to use both narrow and wide focus lenses to assess the groupworker's practice.

When we turn to consider what a partial approach offers the *assessment* of groupwork practice, we can see that it helps to reduce good groupwork practice to its constituent elements, with each aspect examined on its own merits. In place of general judgments about "pass" or "fail," a partial assessment enables a consideration of which parts of the person's groupwork are competent and why, and which are not yet competent, and what specific improvements are needed.

However, the partial approach to assessment of a groupworker's ability has limitations. "Put crudely, it might count and measure every fragment of a cup and find each adequate, yet fail to notice these broken pieces are not a cup" (Doel et al., 2002, p. 38). Assessment of a groupworker's practice must consider *context* and the integration of skills, theory and values (Manor, 2000, p. 209). A rounded assessment of groupwork talents requires a synthesis of the specific and the general, the discrete and the dynamic. A holistic approach to assessing a groupworker's practice therefore encompasses both the partial and the contextual.

How, then, can we put this complex idea into practice? What would an assessment tool look like, one that successfully synthesizes the partial and the whole?

Signposting: A Tool for Learning, Assessment and Research in Groupwork Practice

The general method which the project has developed to help learners gather and present evidence of their abilities in groupwork is a *portfolio*. This term has grown to cover a very wide variety of approaches (Coleman, Rogers, & King, 2002; Taylor, Thomas & Sage, 1999). In the Groupwork Project a dialectical approach has evolved, in which the person compiling the portfolio is encouraged to have a dialogue with him or herself:

> If the portfolio is to be an instrument of both learning and assessment, it needs to be construed as an invitation to a dialogue. It is a discussion

which the learner has with him or herself, a kind of reflective soliloquy. In common with a soliloquy, we all know that this dialogue with oneself, though seemingly private, is held before an audience. It is not just the content which is important, but also the quality of the dialogue as a dialogue. In other words, the assessor looks not just for evidence of specific accomplishments, but also for signs of the author's ability to question and maintain a continuing reflective dialogue. (Doel et al., 2002, p. 50)

Establishing this form of dialogue on a completely blank sheet would be a difficult task. In recognition of this, the program developed questions for the learners to ask themselves; the questions are intended to be relatively open questions, yet focused around specific aspects of the learner's groupwork experiences. The whole portfolio is, therefore, composed of numerous sections which focus on discrete topics, such as "offering the group to individuals," "group themes," "evaluating the group," etc. Within these sections the learner is given the signposts of open questions.

The portfolio establishes a pattern for the groupwork learner of recognition of the difference between a description of what happened, an analysis of why it happened as it did, and a reflection on how it might have happened differently or what the groupworker has learned from the experience. The dialectical questions are, therefore, always grouped into these three forms: Description; Analysis; Reflection (the DAR trilogy, see Figure 6.2).

Unit 5 GROUP PROCESSES

1. Individuals in the group

Description

Using the pen-pictures of the individual group members you completed in Section 1.3, describe the different kinds of role taken by individuals in the group; for example, a person who regularly provided "internal leadership," a person who tended to be scapegoated in the group, etc.

Analysis

Take two examples of behaviours in the group. What meaning do you think the behaviours had for the group, and how was this helpful or hindering? Did you "name" any of these situations (i.e. bring them into the open)—if so, how and why? If not, why?

Reflection

How did the individuals' behaviour in these examples make you feel? If you could script your response how would it differ from the reality of what happened?

Figure 6.2 An Example of the DAR Process

Finally, the questions are framed in clear, direct language. This clarity is not intended to eliminate ambiguity, since this can be very creative, but to enable the compiler of the portfolio to spend more time on their own response rather than struggling to comprehend the question.

The system of signage in the portfolio is work in progress. It is always possible to see how improvements might be made to the quality of the questions, in order to facilitate the reflective dialogue. The compiler of the portfolio is expected to elaborate on the signpost questions, so that the dialogue itself provokes further questions. The significance of the phrasing of questions is illustrated by Caspi and Reid (2002), who consider alternative ways of initiating a dialogue about obstacles in task-centred supervision:

Rather than asking, "Do you see any obstacle that might interfere with your success in carrying out the task?" the issue could be raised in other ways: "What needs to happen for the task to be implemented successfully?" (Caspi & Reid, 2002, p. 265).

Levels of Assessment

The signposting in itself does not indicate an explicit standard of practice. For those groupwork learners who are qualified social workers there is an expectation of greater integration of the groupwork literature and reference to group theory into the text of their portfolios. However, whatever stage in their career, the signposting system actively encourages learners to engage in doubt and uncertainty, and to be honest in their accounts and reflections:

As a groupworker, I have found it difficult to "name" any of the occurrences [of Lily's self-deprecating behaviour], for fear of drawing unwanted attention to Lily, and highlighting her perceived problems. (Groupwork portfolio in Doel et al., 2002, p. 147)

The person assessing the groupwork portfolio has to balance the quality of the dialogue with the quality of the groupwork as revealed through this dialogue. It is fine to have instances of the groupworker's candor about the inadequacy of their response at a particular time, but there would be concern if the portfolio consisted largely of "if only I could have . . ." statements. The portfolio should also provide an opportunity for the learner's groupwork strengths and achievements to shine through. The assessor is looking for a balance between newly acquired understanding and awareness which the groupworker has yet to put into practice, and those areas where the learner has successfully developed new strategies and seen results. The "Learning-Practice Escalator" (see Figure 6.3) portrays the development of a learner's ability from the bottom rung, where there is no awareness of a dilemma or issue in the group, to the top rung, where there is a strategy which is integrated into the learner's regular groupwork practice and which he or she is able to teach to others. This is not to suggest that progress up the ladder is linear and

Strategy taught to others
Strategy fully integrated
Strategy repeated, refined, adapted
Strategy tried and failed
A hypothetical response
No developed response
Awareness of dilemma or issue
Unaware of dilemma or issue

(From Doel et al., 2002, p.148)

Figure 6.3 The LPE (Learning-Practice Escalator)

inevitable; it is likely that any one portfolio will reveal a variety of positions on the ladder.

Portfolios in the Groupwork Project: How Successful Has the Signposted Portfolio Been?

Of the 121 learners in the project (see Figure 6.4), 47 (39%) have so far submitted a portfolio (figures at June 2003). All but eight (17%) of these 47 portfolios were successful on the first submission, though two qualified learners were found to have submitted portfolios which only reached pre-qualifying standard. All eight re-submitted portfolios passed. The number of portfolios will increase a little as those who have recently completed groups continue to compile their evidence of groupwork skills.

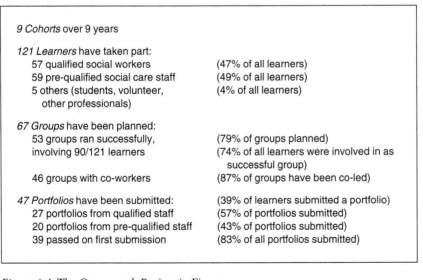

Figure 6.4 The Groupwork Project in Figures

We have no similar statistics with which to compare this project, so it is difficult to judge whether these figures are a remarkable success or an abject failure. Since it is not possible to complete a portfolio without completing a group, we should perhaps consider what percentage of those learners who completed a group also compiled a portfolio: 52% (that is, 47 of the 90 learners who successfully completed a group). This percentage improves to 63% when we consider the percentage of qualified social workers who ran a group to successful completion and compiled a portfolio. Pre-qualified staff in the project were encouraged but not expected to compile a portfolio.

An analysis of the individual cohorts making up the project reveals considerable differences between them. For example, all of the 17 groups planned by learners in Cohort #2 were successful (100%), whilst only five of the nine groups planned in Cohort #5 were successful (55.5 %). Eight of the 13 members of Cohort #4 successfully submitted portfolios (61.5%), whilst only three of the 14 members of Cohort #7 submitted portfolios (21.5%). We have been unable to identify any specific reasons to explain these differences.

The groupwork program requires qualified social workers to complete a portfolio, though this does not guarantee that they do; some move on to other jobs and agencies, and the only sanction for non-submission of portfolio is inability to gain credit towards the post-qualifying award. This sanction has more teeth now that it is related to career and salary progression (see later). Even though there is no such requirement that pre-qualified staff should complete a portfolio, no less than 20 have submitted portfolios, and successfully. This represents 34% of all pre-qualified learners in the project, and 43% of all portfolios presented to the Assessment Panel.

The qualitative success of the signposted portfolio is less easily measured, though the evidence is available to be discovered in each and every portfolio. There is abundant evidence of the development of the learners' own understanding of groupwork, and of the positive impact of the groups on their members. The signposting in the portfolio has undoubtedly had a beneficial effect both on the numbers of learners prepared to undertake the task of collecting and submitting evidence, and on the quality of the observations and reflections elicited. The first question in the *via voce* asks learners how they found the process of compiling the portfolio, and many learners have remarked that they do not think they would have been able to complete the portfolio without the signposting structure. None have commented that the signposting inhibited them.

In particular, the pattern of Description, Analysis and Reflection in each of the sections of the portfolio has proved true to our stated objective of a holistic approach to the assessment of the learner's groupwork: that is, attention to both the partial and the contextual. The range of materials included in the portfolio, which includes videotape, flipcharts, questionnaires and "group logs," in addition to the learner's responses to the questions, provides many different windows on the groupwork undertaken.

Continuing Professional Development (CPD)

The training program which underpins the Groupwork Project is one course in a menu of programs on offer to the staff in the social services agency. As an accredited course carrying 60 post-qualifying credits, it provides onehalf of the total number of credits needed for the Post-Qualifying Award in Social Work (PQSW) in the UK. (These arrangements are currently under review.) The full program of continuing professional development has also recently been linked to the agency's system of career progression; essentially, social workers must complete an element of the post-qualifying program before they are eligible for advancement, and post-qualifying awards are increasingly seen as essential for further progression.

The link between continuing professional development and career progression has undoubtedly become one of the drivers for the Groupwork Project. However, there were nine different programs from which to choose, so we hoped that participants continued to have a primary motivation to do groupwork, rather than solely to do something which brings salary and career advancement. For example, one learner submitted a groupwork portfolio even though he had already achieved the PQSW and had no need for the extra credits.

The Groupwork Project has been a strong influence on the development of the CPD program overall. In part this is because it was one of the first courses to be offered. The signposting system is being transferred to other courses in the overall program. The groups that have been established as a result of the program have had a profound effect on many people's lives, and this is well documented though the stories told in the portfolios. Some of these accounts furnish a book in which the main reference point is the evidence provided by social workers' portfolios of groupwork practice (Doel, 2006).

However, there is a word of caution. The impact on the agency as a whole remains marginal, and this is disappointing. For example, there is little evidence that the groupwork portfolios are read outside the existing circle of learners, and usually by learners who want to see exemplars in order to prepare their own portfolio. The portfolios are available only as hard copies, the new technology is under-developed and communication across and between agencies is clumsy. This wealth of evidence of good practice is not, therefore, known as widely as it should be within the agency itself, and groupwork continues to operate in the agency's penumbra. In this respect, groupwork does not differ from other aspects of social work practice in the context of English social services, little of which surfaces beyond anecdote for the wider world to notice. The signposted portfolio does at least provide an open window on this groupwork practice, should others choose to read and learn.

References

Caspi, J. & Reid, W. J. (2002). *Educational supervision in social work: A task-centered model for field instruction and staff development.* New York: Columbia University Press.

CCETSW (1992). *The requirements for post-qualifying education and training in the personal social services (Paper 31).* London: Central Council for Education and Training in Social Work.

Coleman, H., Rogers, G. & King, J. (2002). Using portfolios to stimulate critical thinking in social work education. *Social Work Education, 21*(5), 583–595.

Doel, M. (2006). *Using groupwork.* London: Routledge/Community Care.

Doel, M. & Sawdon, C. (1995). A strategy for groupwork education and training in a social work agency. *Groupwork, 8*(2), 189–204.

Doel, M. & Sawdon, C. (1999a). No group is an island: Groupwork in a social work agency. *Groupwork, 11*(3), 50–69.

Doel, M. & Sawdon, C. (1999b). *The essential groupworker: Teaching and learning creative groupwork.* London: Jessica Kingsley.

Doel, M. & Sawdon, C. (2002). *Learning, practice and assessment: Signposting the portfolio.* London: Jessica Kingsley.

Doel, M., Sawdon, C. & Morrison, D. (2002). *Learning, practice and assessment: Signposting the portfolio.* London & Philadelphia: Jessica Kingsley.

Hodge, J. (1985). *Planning for co-leadership: A practice guide for groupworkers.* Newcastle, UK: Groupvine.

Manor, O. (2000). *Choosing a groupwork approach: An inclusive stance.* London: Jessica Kingsley.

O'Hagan, K. (ed.) (1996). *Competence in social work practice,* London: Jessica Kingsley.

Sharry, J. (2001). *Solution-focused groupwork.* London: Sage.

Sheldon, B. & Chivers, R. (2000). *Evidence-based social care: A study of prospects and problems.* Lyme Regis, UK: Russell House Publishing.

Taylor, I., Thomas, J., & Sage, H. (1999). Portfolios for learning and assessment: Laying the foundations for continuing professional development. *Social Work Education, 18*(2), 147–160.

Ward, D. (1998). Groupwork. In R. Adams, L. Dominelli & M. Payne (Eds.), *Social work: Themes, issues and debates* (pp. 149–159). London: Macmillan.

Yelloly, M. & Henkel, M. (1995). *Learning and teaching in social work.* London: Jessica Kingsley.

7   The Use of Group Work with New York City Firefighters Post-9/11

John Marchini

Introduction

Group work has been fundamental to the Counseling Service Unit (CSU) of the Fire Department of New York (FDNY) following the devastation of September 11. The diverse needs of the various populations served by the CSU led to the use of many different group work approaches. This chapter will critically examine the use of group work with one particular population: family liaisons.

The firefighters who plunged into the role of family liaison in the wake of September 11 were unprepared for the role before them. The usual procedure when a line of duty death occurs is for the firehouse to "adopt" the family of the fallen firefighter for whatever length of time that the family requests help. The loss of 343 firefighters in the World Trade Center collapse placed a strain on this tradition which had never before been encountered or envisioned.

The response of the FDNY was to relieve at least one firefighter from each directly affected firehouse from his regular duties and assign to him the role of family liaison. The liaisons would be the first point of contact for families for whatever help they required. Their role was an intermediary one that functioned in two main areas: (1) Facilitating the bereaved families' connection with the FDNY Counseling Service Unit's (CSU) professional services and referral system; and (2) Helping the families navigate the complex and arduous logistical terrain of funeral and memorial services, finances, and legal affairs.

It was anticipated that the family liaisons' function would continue through the end of each family's memorial or funeral service when the liaison would then return to his regular duties. It was recognized, however, that the needs of the families would not end there. It was also anticipated that the emotional burden on the family liaisons would continue past these dates.

This chapter will critically examine the use of group work with the family liaisons. It will discuss their needs and issues, identifying commonalities and differences, and show how group work was used to meet those needs and address those issues. Two aspects of the work with family liaisons will be highlighted and illustrated: (1) accelerated movement through phases of group development; and (2) mutual aid.

The chapter will demonstrate how the commonality among the members and their mutual aid tradition lead to an acceleration of the group process so that the first session reflects all the phasic issues of a longer-term group. Below will be reviewed the planning for the group, the significance of mutual aid to the group process, and the actions taken in each phase. The chapter will conclude with the implications of the findings for group work practice.

Planning

Kurland (1978) recognized planning as an essential prerequisite for success of any group. The questions of need, purpose, composition, structure, content, and pregroup contact are also essential to the functioning of any group.

The first group for family liaisons was organized using Kurland's (1978) model of group planning. The need was clearly present. Peer counselors (current or retired firefighters who have had no formal training in counseling) began to report from firehouses in late October, 2001 about family liaisons being overwhelmed and exhausted by their role. Also, calls were coming into the CSU from apprehensive superior officers concerned about the well-being of liaisons in their firehouse. Furthermore, a number of liaisons had personally contacted the CSU due to the "stress" they were suffering. Apart from one informational and logistical meeting convened by the FDNY in late September, there was no formal contact between the family liaisons and the FDNY Administration. Neither was there a structure in place to facilitate the liaisons using each other as resources. This contributed to haphazard and inconsistent methods of obtaining information for their assigned families, and confusion due to the often contradictory nature of the information. It was felt that a group would be the best way of addressing these needs because the interaction between members would permit the sharing of resource knowledge and also provide the needed emotional support.

The purpose of the group was stated as being "To help family liaisons better cope with their role through the creation of an environment safe for discussion of personal experiences of the role and the fostering of mutual aid." The group composition was homogeneous in gender, race, and employment (male, white firefighters). There were 63 firefighters officially in the role of family liaison, although there were more than these informally by the time the group was convened. All were contacted. They indicated a range of responses to their current situation including anger, frustration, and disillusionment toward the Fire Department management, the CSU, and their own firehouses, to pride and satisfaction at their performance given the few tools they began with, to grief, hope, and fulfillment from working with their assigned families. Many felt alone with the task, whereas others spoke of being completely supported by their firehouse.

The group would be co-led by a peer counselor and a social worker from the CSU. The peer counselor would be an initial source of trust and understanding for the members, whilst the social worker would provide process analyses and continual needs assessment. The co-leaders could also be seen as splitting the content and process of the group. The group was to be in a 90-minute open discussion format, allowing the members to talk about what was relevant to their experience as liaison. The pre-group contact involved the co-leaders calling every liaison and inviting him to the group, as well as letters of invitation being sent to all family liaisons. Flyers were sent to all the firehouses in the city and information had been printed in the Union paper and FDNY dispatches. It was anticipated that ten persons might be interested in the group and nine family liaisons had pre-registered. The first group session was held in January 2002 with 22 liaisons showing up.

Mutual Aid

William Schwartz (1961) saw the social work group as "an enterprise in mutual aid, an alliance of individuals who need each other, in varying degrees, to work on certain common problems" (p. 266). The group member forges many and varied relationships within the group, not merely one with the worker or the group as an entity. Mutual aid creates the possibility for the group to advance in ways unthought of by individual members or leaders, and creates an arena for individual change.

Mutual aid does not necessarily arise naturally in groups. The function of the worker is to explore the group process in order to mediate between the individual members and the group. Tasks employed by the worker to this end include searching for common ground between opposing views within the group, contracting, pointing out obstacles to work, sharing information, and modeling to help the members use and trust the group.

Shulman and Gitterman (1994) incorporate mutual aid as an essential factor in their Life Model of social work practice. Northen and Kurland (2001) identify mutual aid as the catalyst for the group becoming a "potent force for development and change" (p. 63). Shulman (1999) identified a number of processes that were indicative of mutual aid, including the sharing of information, mutual support and demand, problem solving, the "all-in-the-same-boat" phenomenon, and the strength-in-numbers phenomenon.

Mutual aid is not expected in the beginning phase of groups since trust and group cohesion have not yet occurred. It is most likely to appear early in single-session or crisis groups, although even in single-session groups, it doesn't show up until the middle of the session (Ebenstein, 1998).

Firefighters are acclimatized to components of mutual aid through firehouse culture. From the use of the word "brother" in referring to a peer, to the lineage that crosses generations within families, the FDNY creates communities of support that extend well beyond the doors of the firehouse. Firefighters and their families often socialize together away from the job: picnics, trips, and parties are common. Major life events such as weddings, births, and christenings have ample firehouse representation. These bonds, solid, nurturing, and durable, create and sustain for firefighters the concept of the firehouse as a second family.

Since firefighters often remain in the same work location for their entire career, firehouses become an organic tribute of mutual aid to the men who work there. Within the walls of every firehouse are gyms, recreation rooms, kitchens, and libraries, all built and maintained by firefighters who are stationed there. This skill and diligence is not confined to the firehouse: if a firefighter needed a new deck in his home, the firehouse would rally without hesitation.

The firehouse culture as just described endowed the family liaisons with superb potential for a successful mutual aid group experience. Their support and care for each other, the ease with which they share information, as well as their ability and willingness to solve problems, can be seen as mutual aid in action. Mutual aid, however, is not merely support. Conflict is the fuel of groups and, unchallenged, a group can easily coast into a safe haven of banality. The demand for work needs to happen, and when the group members cannot demand work from each other, it is the worker who must do so. The worker's role is to mediate the process of the group. When the group finds itself stuck, despite attempts to move forward, the worker must identify the obstacle and demand it be addressed.

Group Phases

The stages of group development have been covered extensively in the literature (Garland, Jones, & Kolodny, 1965; Northen, 1969; Northen & Kurland, 2001; Schwartz, 1971). Although the number of stages and their delineation are debated, the development of the group over time is never in doubt. The movement from one stage to the next is fluid, but the characteristics of the stages are recognizable and predictable (Sarri & Galinsky, 1985). For this reason, the stages of group development are often reduced to three: beginning, middle, and end (Brandler & Roman, 1999).

For the group member, the beginning phase is one of defining the group purpose, trust–mistrust, approach–avoidance, and anxiety. Testing of the worker is common and expected. The middle phase is where the work takes place. Members begin to establish their individual identity and accept the differences of others. Competition and sub-grouping take place, although the group is seen as unique and important to the members. The group purpose is understood and members are able to work together to fulfill this purpose. Endings show the group members communicating freely, even though they are parting from the group. Ambivalence is present: Members can deny the importance of the group by fleeing, or fear leaving it (Brandler & Roman, 1999; Garland, Jones, & Kolodny, 1965; Hartford, 1971; Northen, 1969; Northen & Kurland, 2001; Sarri & Galinsky, 1985; Schwartz, 1971).

Accelerated group phases are most likely to occur in crisis groups and single-session groups. These groups go through beginnings, middles, and ends just as any other group does, however the phases are likely to be accelerated. There are differing views, however, as to the speed of the phase development. Ebenstein (1998) suggests that in such groups a longer time is given to beginnings so that contracting and commonalities be established. Brandler and Roman (1999) claim the opposite: that spending too much time on beginnings is the problem and that the group will move readily into the work phase on sensing the confidence of the worker's abilities.

Beginnings

The following process excerpt is from the first few minutes of the first family liaison group. The interaction took place immediately after the co-leaders had introduced themselves and reviewed the purpose of the group.

WORKER: I think it would be a helpful start to have you guys tell us what your expectations are of this group: What do you want to get from it? How it can be helpful for you?

BILL: [Directly to worker] How long are we going to be off the chart [not scheduled for regular duty assignments]?

MIKE: Are people still off the chart?

SEAN: I'm off the chart.

DAVID : I'm not off the chart . . . I've been working. I speak with Sue [the widow he is a liaison to] everyday.

STEVE: We have a revolving schedule going. We have a few guys who get time off. The lieutenant that did it originally wasn't able to do it, so we all got involved.

ROB: We haven't had anyone off the chart since Thanksgiving. I didn't know guys were still off the chart.

DAVID : Have you guys been using your own cars? What happens with that?

SEAN : You can call the commissary and get transport. We've been doing that.

DAVID: What about expenses?

FRANK: We have a fund we get refunded from.

JIM: Some houses don't have so much money. All the Manhattan houses have money, but the smaller ones don't. That's going to blow up too.

BILL: Yeah, and guys fighting over tickets. That's fucked-up. Men in Hawaii or on cruises who had nothing to do with anything, and us stuck here.

Bill is testing the leader with his first comment, characteristic of the beginning stage of group development. However, the fury of the ensuing interaction is a creative one indicative of the group's rapid transition to the middle stage of group.

Unable to voice the *emotional* impact of the family liaison role, the group members were most vocal about the *operational* difficulties surrounding their role. Contracting and clarification of group purpose by the worker are essential in group beginnings. However, the contract is a living bond, an ongoing endeavor between the worker and the members in every stage of a group. The continuing process shows how the group purpose has an alienating effect on the liaisons.

WORKER: These are certainly big concerns here: getting the time and the logistical support needed to do this job correctly. But we're not here to take care of those kinds of questions now.

BILL: What's the use of this group then? Is this just going to be another meeting where we sit around and talk about what we need and nothing gets done?

WORKER: We're listening to you. We want to know how you are coping.

BILL: How we're coping? What do you think? It's crazy out there. We're with these families all the time, going to [memorial and funeral] services, using up our vacation, trying to get time to see them.

PETE: We're not going to sit around and talk about our feelings, if that's what you want.

What the liaisons experienced from the worker's statement was the very same lack of concern they were battling in their role as liaisons outside of the group.

Within the space of five minutes, the liaisons already were freely expressing anger, frustration, and confusion and had identified as commonalities the operational problems they were encountering. The characteristic beginning theme of testing the leader was present but the group rapidly moved beyond that by setting their own agenda. To understand this rapid development of the group the composition of the group needs to be discussed.

The commonality of experience was a binding factor for group members. Mutual Aid always existed but was never supported by a structure. First, there was the obvious homogeneity of being firefighters, rescuers of others regardless of the very real possibility of danger to themselves. ("We walk into burning buildings when everyone else is running out.") They were white males who had all suffered terrible losses of friends and co-workers. It must also be remembered that their membership of the group was in and of itself a commonality: they had decided that they wanted to help the families of the bereaved.

These commonalities in themselves had the potential to fuel phase advancement, but one final factor gave spark to it. The firefighters who became family liaisons were often men who had an active presence in the firehouse, perhaps as Union Delegate or informal leaders. The effect of this on the group was that a few of the active union members knew almost everyone else in the group, and every group member knew at least one other member. The co-leader was known to many of the men, and the social worker had spoken with all group members by phone. After the 15–20 minutes the liaisons had been together prior to the start of the group, they all knew each other by name; firehouse;

and number of years on the job, which is equally, if not more, important as rank.

Middles

As would be expected, the attention paid to the operational issues raised by the family liaisons led to substantial emotional content in the liaison groups. The emotional content did surface in the middle of the first group, although its intensity was beyond what would normally be expected at such a stage of a group's life. A group member commented on what he thought the workers' expectation of the group was: "You want us to sit around and talk about our feelings. Well, we're not going to do that!" The worker acknowledged the comment and then highlighted the feelings that had been engulfing the group since it had convened: anger, frustration, confusion, and resignation of the group members toward the FDNY upper command.

In the beginning phase of a group, directly identifying and acknowledging such strong affect may elicit defensiveness or withdrawal from the members. Initially, it appeared as such, as the liaisons said nothing and stared dejectedly at the floor, one another, and the workers. Their silence was not, however, one of withdrawal; rather, it buzzed with expectancy as the liaisons processed the information. The silence was broken by the liaisons discussing the guilt they felt in allocating their time since 9/11. Recognizing the comment as indicative of the work of the middle stage allowed the worker to step back from the active leadership role he had expected to take. The expression of affect was a signifier of the group members' willingness to work and, as Schwartz (1971) said, "Without affect there is no investment" (p. 12).

When the worker called the group's attention to the feelings being expressed despite the members' insistence that they did not want to talk about them, he revealed an aspect of the group that had until that moment been unacknowledged. The demand for work was not a demand that the group members immediately talk about their feelings; the demand was that the group recognize and acknowledge the presence of what they had heretofore denied. This demand helped the group express its trepidation when speaking of their own "problems" when they were surrounded by so much death and grief.

The discussion of taboo areas is facilitated through mutual aid. In the first group session, death was conspicuously absent from all discussion until toward the end.

DAVID: Have any of you guys buried parts?

BOB: Yeah, we found a part and that was enough for a burial.

SEAN: All you need is any body part to have a service.

ROBERT: We had a memorial service all planned and two days before it they found him.

DAVID: What happens with that? Do you tell the wife what was found?

MIKE: You just tell them you found enough to have a burial. They're all closed caskets; the funeral director takes care of that.

PETE: What about when more body parts are found? I've heard the department calls up to tell the family each time a new part is found. I wouldn't want my family to go through that.

BILL: You can sign off at the funeral home that you don't want to be informed of any more found pieces. All you need for a Christian burial is a small piece.

Initially, this exchange appeared to be disconnected from the rest of the group process. It followed a discussion on guilt, where members had expressed ambivalence about taking time to take care of their own lives. Also, the language, speaking of "parts" and "pieces," kept the exchange impersonal, concrete, and unemotional: a deadening contrast to the prior discussion

Looking at the exchange through the eyes of mutual aid, however, revealed a more unified vista. The members had been both gradually exploring more difficult themes throughout the session and increasingly demonstrating a wider range of affect. When David asked if anyone had buried any parts, he felt safe presenting a taboo subject to a group that had already tolerated discussion of members' guilt, anger, and frustration. The dialectic process of mutual aid had built each new expression of affect on those already revealed and accepted. David knew that the liaisons were "all-in-the-same-boat" and that made the group the proper place to ask his question.

From these and previous examples, mutual aid is seen in a number of ways: sharing information, dialectical process, entering taboo areas, the all-in-the-same-boat phenomenon, mutual support, mutual demand, and the strength-in-numbers phenomenon.

In subsequent groups, the members continued to do middles work. Group members were able to risk vulnerability and show their strengths; an increasing ability to problem solve together was present. The fifth session was a psychoeducational workshop on the process of grief and bereavement presented by professionals in this field. The presenters got 15 minutes into their work, when a few poignant questions from the liaisons led to a more in-depth discussion of the topic than had been anticipated. The cohesion of the group allowed members to request precisely what information they required; they were fully participating in the meeting of their own needs. In this action they once again were able to demonstrate how they retained the control of the group process addressing it to their collective needs.

The positive effect of group cohesion has been discussed extensively in the literature (Hartford, 1971; Shulman & Gitterman, 1994; Schwartz, 1971; Yalom, 1995). A sense of togetherness, pride and satisfaction from being in the group, and the ability to act as a group, all signs of group cohesion, were prominently displayed by the members.

Endings

The group ending did not conform to standard descriptions of this phase. A number of group formats were utilized over the seven-month duration of the group. It should be noted that mutual aid of the intensity seen in these groups also has a cost. Here the devotion to their role as family liaison leads to an inadvertent separation from their own families. One of the recurring themes was enmeshment: the liaisons had often been spending more time with the families of the bereaved than with their own families. Thus consistent with ending the group members need to look outward once again. With this in mind, the group was moved to a Dude Ranch in the Catskills for the weekend. Liaisons were invited to attend, all expenses paid, with their own immediate family. CSU counselors also attended with their own families. Effective modeling was helpful in a way that suggestions could never be. Formal counseling over the weekend consisted of one 90-minute group each for the liaisons and their spouses. Suggesting that the liaisons spend more time with their kids was never as effective as transporting the whole family to a place where there was nothing to do but relax.

Conclusion and Implications

A few words need to be said about worker authenticity before concluding. As in any tight-knit community, the firefighters of the FDNY have their own culture. Their shared history, both immediate and generational, creates a language, sense of humor, morality, and deviance that is always present in their self-awareness as firefighters. Entering any such community can be fearful, but working with the FDNY post-9/11 shows how one of the basic tenets of social work ensures the fear is dealt with appropriately.

Authenticity demands truth from the worker and in return gives freedom. In introducing himself to the family liaison group, the worker said he was not a firefighter and would not for an instant pretend to know what they were going through. He told them that he was, however, an experienced group worker, which meant that he knew how to help them help themselves.

This chapter has examined the interconnection between two aspects of group work—how pre-existing mutual aid fostered accelerated group phase development—and shown their importance in group work with family liaisons with the FDNY. However, flexibility was also an important part played by the worker. Worker flexibility, although an important aspect of all group work, was shown to be necessary around the group formats offered and the negotiation of the contract. It was shown that the flexibility of the worker added to the functioning of the group through the members' trust of the workers and mutual aid. The group was always in the middle phase of existence. The commonalities of the members, including vocation, shared history, and similar character traits, helped this tremendously. The commonalities also increased the occurrence of mutual aid in the group. The firehouse culture had primed the liaisons to be available to this, as well as the disaster they had been through.

Although this chapter does not reflect a research study, some follow-up and anecdotal reports helped in evaluating the impact of this group on the members. Two months after the first anniversary of 9/11, phone calls and meetings with around 30 of the group members reported that they had found the group helpful in three areas:

1.   Forming an informal network with other liaisons for the exchange of information and support;
2.   Helping them separate from the families they were working with in a way that did not cause the liaisons to feel guilt about abandoning the families; and
3.   Helping the liaisons reconnect with their own families.

Just as in crisis work it is important to recognize the depth of the bond between group members. When working with a group that are already bonded to each other in a mutual aid tradition one needs to recognize that it will lead to a far more rapid movement into the middle phase work.

References

Brandler, S. & Roman, C. (1999). *Group work: Skills and strategies for effective interventions* (2nd ed.). Binghamton, NY: Haworth Press.

Ebenstein, H. (1998). Single-session groups: issues for social workers. *Social Work with Groups, 21*(1/2), 49–60.

Garland, J. A., Jones, H. E., and Kolodny, R. L. (1978). A model for stages of development in social work groups. In S. Bernstein (Ed.), *Explorations in group work: Essays in theory and practice* (pp. 17–71). Boston, MA: Boston University School of Social Work.

Gitterman, A. & Shulman, L. (1994). *Mutual aid groups, vulnerable populations and the life cycle* (2nd ed.). New York: Columbia University Press.

Hartford, M. E. (1971). *Groups in social work.* New York: Columbia University Press.

Kurland, R. (1978). Planning: The neglected component of group development. *Social Work with Groups, 1*(2), 173–178.

Northen, H. (1969). *Social work with groups.* New York: Columbia University Press.

Northen, H. & Kurland, R. (2001). *Social work with groups* (3rd ed.). New York: Columbia University Press.

Sarri, R. C. & Galinsky, M. J. (1985). A conceptual framework for group development. In M. Sundel, P. Glasser, R. C. Sarri & R. Vinter (Eds.), *Individual change through small group* (pp. 70–86). New York: Free Press.

Schwartz, W. (1961). *Social work: The collected writings of William Schwartz.* Itasca, IL: F. E. Peacock Publishers, Inc.

Schwartz, W. (1971). On the use of groups in social work practice. In W. Schwartz and S. Zalba (Eds.), *The practice of group work* (pp. 3–24). New York: Columbia University Press.

Shulman, L. (1999). *The skills of helping individuals, families, groups, and communities* (4th ed.). Itasca, IL: F. E. Peacock Publishers, Inc.

Shulman, L. and Gitterman, G. (1994). The life model, mutual aid, oppression, and the mediating function. In A. Gitterman, A. & L. Shulman (Eds.), *Mutual aid groups: Vulnerable populations, and the life cycle* (2nd ed.), (pp. 3–28). New York: Columbia University Press.

Yalom, I. (1995). *The theory and practice of group psychotherapy* (4th ed.). New York: Basic Books.

8 Support Groups for Welfare Moms

Evelyn F. Slaght

Introduction

Welfare reform has heralded in a new age in which poor women on welfare are expected to be employed and to perform their parenting responsibilities regardless of the circumstances that brought them to the welfare office in the first place. Many are finding the multiple demands overwhelming. The current focus of the social service system is on carrying out policy related to the Personal Responsibility and Work Opportunity Act of 1996 (PRWORA—soon to be reauthorized). Often workers are so preoccupied with helping women meet the work mandates that they fail to provide the emotional supports needed to gain confidence in searching for and maintaining a job and handling parenting duties and personal crises.

Job preparation and training will most likely continue to be the primary responsibility of the agency worker, but small facilitated groups (TANF—Temporary Assistance for Needy Families—groups) can be organized to provide a system of peer support that will improve significantly the success of these moms. TANF groups should offer both parenting and personal supports as well as assistance with task accomplishments related to securing employment and job retention, and in so doing, insure that PRWORA's goal of self-sufficiency is achieved.

Purpose

Consistent with the goal of PRWORA, the primary purpose of TANF support groups must be work-related, including such activities as critiquing resumes and role-playing in preparation for job interviews. These types of activities will be far less threatening in front of one's peers, but a professionally trained social work facilitator will be needed to guide the group process. As group members obtain jobs, the focus of the group should shift to increasing the ability of the TANF mom to cope with new parenting pressures and other emotional stressors related to the demands associated with working full time. A major advantage of TANF groups is that members can assist one another in arriving at ways to balance the new work and family demands often more effectively than other support mechanisms because the members are intimately familiar with what each other is experiencing. As process groups, they can provide outlets for expressions of the fear, anger, and frustration associated with the multiple responsibilities.

The justification for TANF support groups to address personal as well as parenting and job-related issues is well substantiated in the literature. Research by the Social Research and Development Corporation (Berlin, Bancroft, Card, Lin, & Robin, 1998) confirms that most TANF applicants come into the public assistance system at a time of crisis in their lives, when help with personal problems is essential.

There are a wide range of personal and parenting problems that may interfere with job search and maintenance, only some of which are acknowledged by the system. For example, in most states, exemptions to the work requirements are not allowed for a mom who has a child with special needs, or for a mom in recovery, or one who was abandoned recently by her significant other. The most common exemption is women who have been victims of domestic violence.

The burdens associated with sudden, single parenthood need to be addressed, especially if violence was involved, given the effect that witnessing this violence may have had on the children. Additionally the stigma that is associated with single-parenthood may require attention. The rejection by the father of the mother and her child(ren) can significantly damage her self-esteem. Such a demoralizing experience can reduce her belief in her ability to secure employment and perform on the job. A group of her peers can be empathetic, and with proper leadership, help to restore her self-confidence.

Other personal problems can interfere with successfully obtaining employment. Seccombe (1999) points out the problems faced by women with criminal records. The story of Kate, who has a criminal record as a consequence of a domestic violence incident, is compelling. Arrested because she attempted to defend herself, she is puzzled by the apparent contradiction that tells her, on the one hand, that she should not be aggressive in relationships, and on the other, that she will need to be assertive if she is to make it in the competitive work world. She finds prospective employers and the social service system unsympathetic to the circumstances that resulted in her criminal record. She learns that she can only depend on family and friends for support and understanding. If Kate comes into the TANF system, she probably will benefit more from a facilitated support group than individual counseling. Without support with personal issues, her chances of achieving self-sufficiency are significantly reduced.

Most corporations today acknowledge the impact of personal problems on job performance. This understanding was the basis for the creation of Employee Assistance Programs. Providing assistance with personal issues can be justified as a job-related service.

Individual advocacy on one's own behalf is a skill that may impact employment, and consequently is a skill applicable to TANF support groups.

Educational and vocational training remediation is not routinely available, but with the help of the TANF support group, members may be willing to acknowledge their educational and training needs and approach the system to secure services. On the other hand, systemic advocacy relative to needed changes in the TANF program must be put aside initially. After basic needs are met through employment, however, TANF recipients can be empowered to address community change and system reform. In the early stages as process groups, however, individual socioemotional needs should take priority. *The worker must recognize, however, that, while her agenda is driven by the agency goals and prioritizing of client needs, the agenda at any given meeting must be client-driven.*

Strategies and Techniques

Considerable planning is required to compose TANF groups, and it is essential that participation be voluntary. Support groups by their nature require that the participants be interested and committed to mutual assistance (Toseland & Rivas, 2001).

Community-based Emphasis

Voluntary participation is made easier when community facilities are used for group meetings. Finding a church or recreation center convenient for the moms is a first step in planning. A community-based approach allows for members to provide continued support after termination. For example, one outcome of the group may be that members periodically assist one another with childcare in cases of emergency or illness. Geographic proximity is essential if this support is to occur.

If the support group is to move beyond emotional support and self-advocacy to developing community resources, again, a community-based approach is necessary. For example, one agency in Maryland worked with a group of clients to help them establish their own businesses. Two of the woman worked together to develop a taxi service in response to the need for transportation for working women in the area.

Recruitment

Making the groups community-based will affect composition since those most accessible to the facility will be most likely to participate. Therefore, if homogeneity is to be respected in composing the groups, it may be necessary to anticipate a need for several groups. If only one or two groups can be run at a time, there should be provisions for a waiting list for those who do not "fit" with the membership of the initial groups. Homogeneous membership may also be achieved by having agency staff refer, but outreach into the community will still be necessary to solicit member involvement and participation. If potential participants feel that this is just one more TANF requirement, it will inhibit their participation and involvement in the group process.

Composition

Homogeneity in composition must take into account basic demographics, such as age, marital status, educational levels, and life style preferences. Because a woman has children does not mean that she is committed to a heterosexual life style, and these differences must be respected. Teens who have children and are part of TANF grants have very different needs than the traditional adult single mom raising her children alone. Respecting commonalities in composing groups is critical to developing cohesion and mutuality (Northen & Kurland, 2001).

The policy changes that have come about through PRWORA combined with changes in the problems presented by TANF moms must be considered in forming TANF support groups. For example, not all TANF recipients are required to work. In every state, provisions are made for those special cases that are exempt from the work requirement. Moms required to work should be in separate groups from those who are exempt, because work-related agenda will not need to be a priority for the exempt group.

More and more grandparents are applying for and receiving TANF when they assume responsibility for their kin. These relatives should have their own groups since their issues are very different.

A positive name for the group that reflects its intended membership should be developed to assist in recruitment and in building cohesive bonds between members. For example, to recruit the traditional single mom on TANF, the worker may wish to title the group, "Single Moms Making it Work." On the other hand, for grandmothers and other relatives who want to take advantage of support groups, the worker may want to advertise "Kin caring for kids"(K4K) groups by posting notices around the neighborhood. Cohen (1995) provides guidelines for GAMA groups (Grandmothers as Mothers Again) which may be helpful. It may even be feasible to develop "Hi, I'm Home" (HiH) groups that can work with parents whose children are in foster care or who have left their children with relatives.

Parents with children in foster care cannot be ignored since their numbers are swelling, according to Bernstein (2002). They will be the hardest to attract because of the stigma associated with what may be viewed as child abandonment. They can overcome the major obstacles to getting their children back, with the help of other mothers whose children are also in foster care, but the group facilitator will need to reassure members about the confidential nature of the group *and that the agenda will be client-driven.* Otherwise, the members will resist sharing negative behaviors and feelings, fearing that this will be reported and jeopardize their chances of reunion. Nonetheless, the child welfare worker should assist by identifying potential

HiH group members, and the group facilitator should maintain contact with the child welfare worker so that as crises arise (court hearings, etc.), the group worker can be alerted and plan for discussion around the issue. Middle-stage meetings in fact may begin with, "Before we begin tonight, are there any new developments in the status of each of your cases?" Weil and Finegold (2002) confirm that additional case management responsibility must be assumed when working with cases where CPS is involved.

Getting agency support to organize and staff HiH groups under TANF auspices may be met with resistance because TANF moms usually lose public assistance when their children are removed from the home. These groups should be considered part of TANF's responsibilities, however, since the CPS mom's ability to resume parenting and obtain employment relieves a significant financial burden on the agency. In this case, the TANF administration can then take credit for enabling one more mom to achieve self-sufficiency. Unfortunately TANF workers and CPS workers do not necessarily work together effectively on these cases; mutual responsibility for a student intern may improve these relationships. *There should be agreement from the beginning on the agenda that the intern will follow, understanding that this must be flexible and vary with the needs of the moms.*

One of the major problems with PRWORA currently is that, when women are sanctioned and/or are dropped from TANF rolls because they reach the time limits without securing employment, there is no follow-up regarding the welfare of the children (Rome & Slaght, 1999). The availability of support groups can insure some level of follow-up, even if informal. The group worker/intern is in a good position to obtain information on the welfare of children whose parents have been sanctioned or returned from foster care. Maintaining community trust prevents the group worker from using this information in anything but a confidential way, but allows for some degree of understanding about the impact of current welfare policy. *Mutual sharing of information between TANF and CPS staff can document some of the hazards of current policy and might force a reexamination of the extent to which our current welfare policy is harmful to children.*

Worker's Role

Social work student interns are the most logical source of staffing for TANF support groups; they will be viewed as less threatening than other professional agency personnel and can utilize their generalist skills. They must be trained, however, to understand how to balance agency goals relative to self-sufficiency with group members' needs for emotional support. *Where CPS cases are concerned, they must recognize that "good parenting" requires that mom feel emotionally supported as well.*

The job-related aspect of the TANF group process may require that the group worker develop skills not normally associated with the social work intern role, such as how to conduct a job search, and prepare and maintain a family budget, along with concrete skills related to parenting issues, such as how to prepare quick and nutritional meals. They also need to understand when it is appropriate to invite experts into the group as part of the educational agenda.

Focus

Work-related agenda

Inasmuch as the proposal for funding for TANF support groups is to come through the welfare system, it is understood that the early agenda of the TANF support groups should focus on members helping each other obtain jobs. This may include discussions on how to read want ads, prepare a resume, and approach a job interview.

Other job-related agenda may include:

- Using the computer to job search;
- Dress and decorum on the job;
- How to cope with tyrannical bosses or bossy co-workers;
- How to cope with discrimination;
- Learning new skills;
- Handling legitimate absences from the job.

Once they are employed, additional agendas may include budget management, child care, and transportation. Time management as a general topic will also need to be covered. While the TANF worker is responsible for making child care, medical coverage, and transportation vouchers available, accessing these resources is not always easy, and the TANF group worker will need to facilitate discussion around some of the frustrations that arise.

In some cases, group members can assist each other with job-related training. For example, computer skills are sometimes more easily learned from a colleague than a professional trainer. Goldberg & Collins (2001) make a strong case for the training needs of TANF recipients, and the use of mentoring which can come from support groups.

Parenting issues

Children unaccustomed to having a working mom may have problems adjusting to child care, and newly working moms may need help coping with getting children to child care and themselves to work on time. Medical problems may arise that interfere with working and parenting.

Other parenting agenda items may include:

- How to locate suitable day care;
- How to synchronize day care and public transportation;

- How to cope with the finicky eater;
- When emergency medical attention is needed and how to access it.

Discussion of parenting issues should recognize that there is no such thing as a perfect parent. The group worker is not there to teach how to be good parents, but rather to enable working mothers to provide each other with emotional supports in coping with the normal problems associated with parenting.

Personal issues

Agenda around personal concerns such as "dating" may arise, and group workers should be prepared to give members permission to discuss such sensitive issues, even though they may not be directly related to getting a job. The Bush administration has taken a strong "pro-family" approach in debates around reauthorization of PRWORA.

Therefore, discussions around partnering and marriage can be legitimized, but it is important to respect the self-determination of the group members and not promote marriage as the single solution, either personally or financially.

On a personal level, the agenda may include:

- Dating and its effects on children;
- Handling the ex-spouse or ex-significant other;
- Drug and alcohol use;
- Seeking and working with other role models for your children;
- Nurturing yourself as well as your child.

It is important to focus on the mom's emotional needs and recognize that she will probably not be a better parent until some of her intra- and inter-personal issues are addressed. TANF moms have the right to be nurtured. As they feel this support, they will be better able to nurture their children.

Many young mothers suffer from depression, brought on by the burden of parenting, the loneliness associated with having no partner, and the pressures of working. The support group must provide an atmosphere where any and all of these pressures can be addressed.

Community-related agenda

Some of the problems of parenting are associated with the lack of resources in the community, especially when schools are inadequate and there are insufficient child care and recreation facilities. Discussions of how to meet the educational and recreational needs of children and families may alter the focus of the group and move it from emotional support to resource development, but in the later stages of the group, this may be necessary, *and should be pursued if members are interested.*

The use of groups to develop community activities and resources is supported by Alvarez and Cabbil (2001). Mondros (2001) offers a number of suggestions on how to use groups to "build resourceful communities."

This suggests the following agenda for TANF groups:

- How to expand day care resources in the neighborhood;
- How to expand recreation resources in the neighborhood;
- How to expand transportation options.

Allowing for these agenda is consistent with Kaplan's(2001) emphasis on balancing task and process in groups.

Evaluation

The primary focus of the group should remain work-related, and should drive the evaluation plan, consistent with the goals of the TANF program. It should be recognized, however, that job performance is affected by personal crises and personal change, and evaluation of the program should include the degree to which these objectives are also achieved. Understanding the relationship between job stability and emotional stability as factors in achieving self-sufficiency will support the development of services under TANF auspices. To measure only the job-related accomplishments without understanding why some moms succeed while others do not is to relegate TANF to a financial service rather than a social service or pro-family program.

A pre-test must be designed and administered prior to the start of the group that examines potential job success followed by a post-test that documents employment outcomes, including job satisfaction and retention. This should include measures of attitudes towards work, initial confidence relative to their ability to get and keep a job, and an assessment of their job skills.

The extent to which the group members anticipate that personal and parenting issues will interfere with employment must be measured as part of the pre-test. Confidence in parenting and personal coping skills should then be examined in the post-test. It can reasonably be assumed that *changes in personal confidence and successful job performance can be measured* across the life of the group, and these changes can be attributed to the effectiveness of the group in contributing to self-sufficiency and self-efficacy.

Additionally, satisfaction with the resources available to group members, especially day care, transportation, and training resources should be measured at the post-test level. Job success is expected to depend on these resources, and no matter how well the group supports members' use of resources, their availability will be a factor in job success.

Social workers cannot be satisfied with simply helping clients obtain employment if it is at the expense of the well-being of the children (Rome & Slaght, 1999); therefore the evaluation must demonstrate that obtaining and maintaining employment has not been at the expense of child welfare. The overall emotional well-being of both mother and child must be included in the program assessment. Schools are in a good position to assess children's response to changing family circumstances and may be helpful in assessing the child's well-being before and after the mother's employment.

CPS should be responsible for maintaining records on all clients with any TANF experience, and follow up to document that the TANF experience, in particular, for those who participated in support programs, was helpful in preventing future abuse and neglect.

Termination

Because of the time limits set by PRWORA, TANF support groups will need to be closed groups. Termination of the group will not necessarily coincide with finding a job. It may need to continue in order to provide support in sustaining employment and surviving on the income that the mom receives from that job. Ideally, the group should end only when the majority of the members have stabilized their employment situations. If student interns are used as facilitators, the life of the group will be limited to the academic year. This is not to say that the group will necessary terminate when the agency facilitator terminates. Rather groups can reorganize and move on, as is suggested by Schopler and Galinsky (1995). A model for this approach is apparent in self-help groups such as Alcoholics Anonymous, currently in vogue in dealing with substance abuse. For example, the social work intern may begin, as the group reaches termination, to develop the indigenous leadership in the group so that the group can continue beyond the social work facilitator's availability. The facilitators' responsibility in this case is to help the group transition from an agency-affiliated group to a self-help group.

Conclusions

TANF support groups can be an important tool in helping clients obtain stable employment and self-sufficiency, thereby meeting the goal of PRWORA. Every aspect of the group experience should, in the final analysis, contribute to successful employment. If in the process clients are also empowered both as parents and personally, this should not only be applauded *but expected*, and the relationship between personal well-being and employment success will be demonstrated. If a task group emerges from this experience, it should be considered a plus. For example, it may result in the development of a client advisory group that could work with the agency to help make TANF programs more relevant to client needs. In the final analysis, the mission of self-sufficiency must be judged not only from the standpoint of whether it saves the government money, but whether it supports the families and children it is intended to serve.

References

Alvarez, A. R. & Cabbil, L. M. (2001). The MELD program: Promoting personal change and social justice through a year-long multicultural group experience. *Social Work with Groups, 24*(1), 3–18.

Berlin, G., Bancroft, W., Card, D., Lin, W., & Robin, P. K. (1998). *Do work incentives have unintended consequences?* Canada: Social Research and Demonstration Corporation.

Bernstein, N. (2002). Side effect of welfare law: The no-parent family. *New York Times* July 29, 151 (52194), A1.

Cohen, C. S. (1995). Making it happen: From great idea to successful support group program. In M. J. Galinsky & J. H. Schopler (Eds.), *Support groups: current perspectives on theory and practice* (pp. 67–80). New York: The Haworth Press.

Goldberg, G. S. & Collins, S. D. (2001). *Washington's new Poor Law: Welfare "reform" and the roads not taken.* New York: The Apex Press.

Kaplan, C. (2001). The purposeful use of performance in groups: A new look at the balance of task and process. *Social Work with Groups, 24*(2), 47–66.

Mondros, J. B. (2001). Building resourceful communities: A group worker's guide to community work. In T. B. Kelly, T. Berman-Rossi, & S. Palombo (Eds.), *Group work: Strategies for strengthening resiliency* (pp. 36–51). New York: The Haworth Press.

Northen, H. & Kurland, R. (2001). *Social work with groups* (3rd Ed.). New York: Columbia University Press.

Rome, S. H. & Slaght, E. F. (1999). Welfare reform and the future of foster care. In J. J. Stretch, M. Bartlett, W. J. Hutchison, S. A. Taylor, J. Wilson (Eds.), *Raising our children out of poverty* (pp. 21–36). New York: The Haworth Press.

Schopler, J. H. & Galinsky, M. J. (1995). Expanding our view of support groups as open systems. In M. J. Galinsky & J. H. Schopler (Eds.), *Support groups: Current perspectives on theory and practice* (pp. 3–10). New York: The Haworth Press.

Seccombe, K. (1999). *So you think I drive a Cadillac.* Boston: Allyn & Bacon.

Toseland, R. W. & Rivas, R. F. (2001). *An introduction to group work practice.* Boston: Allyn & Bacon.

Weil, A. & Finegold, K. (2002). *Welfare reform: The next Act.* Washington, DC: The Urban Institute Press.

9 Mask Making and Social Groupwork

Nuala Lordan, Deirdre Quirke, and Mary Wilson

Introduction

Social work is a professional endeavour, which focuses on the process of understanding other people. Social work is not a fixed activity; the rules are continually changing and shift with the meanings and the motives current in society. The double bind that currently confronts the profession rests on the need to reconcile and respond to the public scrutiny aspect of practice with the humanistic ideals on which the profession was developed. "Social work is quintessentially a humanist activity. In a society that is increasingly materialistic and governed in terms of economic rather than social values, humanism is challenged as never before" (Powell, 1999, p. 14).

In addition to posing challenges post-modernism offers new paradigms for constructing social work. For example social work practitioners have a vast practice wisdom, which has not as yet been recognised as contributing to the dominant discourse. As social work educators we place a high value on the practice wisdom of practitioner/participants, recognising the multi-faceted nature of knowledge and the consequences arising from the dominance of didactic approaches. We have a strong belief in the equality of intuitive and cognitive processes and endeavour to integrate them in an inclusive pedagogy. Our quest as educators is to produce reflective and reflexive practitioners who can respond creatively within a world of increased chaos, uncertainty and fragmentation. "Human beings possess a range of capacities and potentials—multiple intelligences—that, both individually and in consort, can be put to many productive uses" (Gardner, 1999, p. 4). Groupwork is a means of connecting with people's intuitive and creative abilities, while offering an alternative to the more constraining features of the educational system. "There is 'an art in gathering together', along with some 'science' in our understanding of what can help or hinder this process" (Douglas, 1983, in Doel & Sawdon, 1999, p. 12).

As social work educators we endeavour to construct learning environments that facilitate self-awareness through questioning and contribute to the discovery of solutions using empowering techniques. As *use of self* is central to professional formation, Wayne and Cohen have suggested that "Social work education groups are called for when the nature of the new information brings questions, anxieties and concerns that need to be addressed for the new knowledge to be useful and valuable" (Wayne & Cohen, 2001, p. 37). Groupwork is an ideal forum for the deconstruction of received wisdom and its reconstruction as new knowledge. "Deconstruction is a series of techniques which enable one to identify and make visible the original premises. Such techniques enable us to envisage ways of disrupting the dominant discourse" (Parker & Shotter, 1990, p. 209, in Pease & Fook, 1999, p. 13). We believe that it is essential to focus on people's intuitive senses, which are so much to the fore in their interactions with each other. The discussion of intuition in the literature has many faces: the difficulties in these interpretations "is not [that there is any inherent lack of validity . . . but [*there is* a] lack of any discussion about the philosophical or practical implications of the use of such intuition" (England, 1983, p. 43).

The focus of the experience outlined here is primarily on the creative *use of self* in social work education and implications for practice. Our aims are to teach social groupwork, to explore the "giving and receiving" of support, and to facilitate the development of greater self-awareness, all of which are core social work skills. Using social groupwork as means and method in professional formation is acknowledged by the view that:

> Groupwork is a potentially integrating experience. It connects the universal experience of being human . . . groups can provide a more effective environment to experience empowerment because they can be used to replicate or simulate the larger society; in many respects they are microcosms of the wider society. (Doel & Sawdon, 1999, p. 13)

Groupwork can draw people together, to explore ways of being and experience non-oppressive relationships. It diversifies and validates different forms of expression by fostering a co-operative approach to problem-solving and supports people working in partnership. "Through creative acts, participants discover themselves as both familiar and strange. Moving beyond language and cultural conventions, a new awareness arises of one's own limitations, also of novel avenues of expression and communication" (Luedemann, 2003, p. 28). Being in a new paradigm requires new responses. In this way questioning of the established hegemony is facilitated and alternative worldviews evolve. Groupwork provides a forum in which both the personal and the political dimension of social work education and practice can be examined. For this to be achieved the goal of facilitation seeks to link the personal experience of participants to an understanding of current political reality. Social work is never value-free nor does it seek to define the experience of another group. By valuing the diversity of narratives or life stories, the postmodern perspective encourages us to review our political beliefs and positions. "As social workers, we should question how our cultural experience might cause us to privilege some aspects of reality and marginalise and disqualify others. We should encourage clients to collaborate in the construction of meaning associated with their experience" (Pozatek, 1994, p. 399, in Pease & Fook, 1999, p. 11).

Mask making involves the use of metaphor, which illuminates personal encounters with a political context. Many groupwork authors have criticised the polarity of personal healing and social change, suggesting instead the importance that they co-exist (Breton, 1995; Cohen & Mullender, 2003; Lordan and Wilson, 2002; Middleman & Wood, 1990; Schwartz, 1971). The view that personal healing and social change are dialectically related, interactive, and inseparable is summed up by Breton who identifies "the essential unity of the personal and the political/social" (Breton, 2002, p. 27).

Mask making has been known and used in many societies. Culturally, it has a well-established place in the performance of ritual. For example, the Mende people of West Africa make very beautiful masks to mark the transition from girlhood to womanhood, which conceal the destructive processes involved by the genital mutilation of women. At the other end of the spectrum, W. B. Yeats used the mask in his plays and poetry to explore cultural and spiritual issues in Irish history (Albright, 1990). "Masks are primordial forms of human expression and human communication. They are found in all cultures and their deployment is as old as humanity itself. This is why masks make excellent vehicles for creative work" (Luedemann, 2003, p. 29). Mask making as a tool can facilitate participants to explore a range of issues encompassing the psychosocial and socio-political realities of people's lives. It can be used as a means of concealing and revealing different aspects of existence. For example, the need to *keep face* or *save face* may manifest defence mechanisms used by individuals in dealing with the complexities in the various arenas they encounter. In social work practice, it may be represented by *defensive practice*, which is a response to the public scrutiny that requires professionals to operate in open, transparent and accountable ways. Mask making as an educational and developmental tool has the potential to begin to unmask some of these processes. The use of the mask in social work education offers opportunities and poses new challenges in addressing the post-modern dilemma of chaos and uncertainty that are everyday events in the lives of social workers and service users. "Rational (scientific) thinking and intuitive (artistic) thinking are both required if we are to be creative in our search for unique responsive solutions" (Lordan, 1996, p. 63).

We have chosen to reflect on working with three groups of experienced social work practitioners. Each group consisted of between 12 and 14 participants. The focus for these groups was on *encountering one's identity and being in relation to the other*. The rationale for choosing this focus was to facilitate participants to reflect on their personal and professional selves as *givers* and *receivers*. "Being where the other person is—is perhaps the most important ethical principle in social work—students need diversified ways of learning about the depth and meaning of this principle and the attitude it implies" (Gronning & Fougner, 2002, p. 105). Each group had different goals in undertaking the mask making. One group was focussed on looking at themselves as practice teachers in relation to their students on fieldwork practice placement. In the second and third groups, members were reflecting on themselves as social workers working directly with service users. The examination of power differentials involved in these situations was an explicit aim of both groups. Group members were drawn from two different social work training courses in our institution. Both were post-graduate programmes, one focussed on training fieldwork practice teachers and the other provided professional training for experienced practitioners. The common characteristics of the groups were that participants were adult learners with considerable life as well as practice experience. Social work education dictates the discourse, mask making provides the tool and the student group is the context in which experiential learning takes place.

Scripting the Process

To begin at the beginning, we provide simple everyday materials such as Vaseline, water, Clingfilm, paint, coloured pieces of cloth and gypsum. With these tools participants are invited to engage in a process of creative experiential groupwork that results in making a mask with and for each other. This process requires the completion of a number of tasks involving the action, reflection, dialogue, and action cycle (Freire, 1970; Kolb, 1984). These take place in sequence and are interwoven with the stages of the groupwork process. This process is, of itself, influenced by many factors such as race, gender, class, ability, culture and religion in addition to prior levels of trust and experiences of participants. The use of an emancipatory approach to groupwork is strongly underpinned by the value base of the facilitators. We are committed to empowerment as means and method of intervention and the deconstruction of power relations in both the micro and macro arenas. In this regard our first prerequisite is to clarify our value base as facilitators.

The principles we aspire to are encapsulated under the title of Meitheal, which is derived from the ancient Gaelic tradition of co-operation and mutual support within communities. Thus it is most apposite as a means of uniting and reclaiming concepts of social justice, human rights and structural oppression. There are a number of principles that underpin the Meitheal approach. First is the need to recognise that the multifaceted nature of the person within a holistic framework is acknowledged. This recognition rests on the intrinsic belief that every human being is uniquely valuable. This social construction of the person is embedded in citizenship and human rights. In addition to this the positive potential and strengths of each individual are acknowledged. This view asserts that individuals have capacities, which when validated, locate and tap the wellsprings of their personal power. People thrive in an environment where the worth of their contributions is recognised and utilised.

Creative/Writing

Creativity is an essential human aspiration and achievement. It has the power to transcend familiar reality and leads us to explore and encounter the unknown and its possibilities (Giddens & Reimer, 1999). Everyone has the ability to create. New ideas and ways of dealing with our world can be discovered and developed by creatively combining dialogue and aesthetic practices. Research suggests that aesthetic education can become a form of critical literacy to empower people to read and name their world (Elias, Jones, & Normie, 1995). Working together in a group is the core activity of the Meitheal. This is the context in which new interpretations are constructed and new solutions emerge. People in the group work together to achieve their aims when passion and hope ignite the fires of change. The group process connects with participants' prime concerns and liberates the energy that has been socially deconstructed. The structure and the process of the group are integrally connected with identifying the wider political implications of participants' experiences. In this milieu the person makes connections between their experiences of reality and the political context in which they are located. This allows for the de-construction of power relationships and assists with the development of action strategies that redress the balance of power. Step by step, choice and action are achieved through reflection and dialogue as a means of generating an all-encompassing helix for transformation.

Beginning Phase

The process is introduced by inviting the participants to engage in a relaxation exercise. The purpose of this is to enable group members to tune in, centre on the here and now and focus on the goals of the workshop. The value of relaxation is well documented as a means of centring one's thoughts, and developing self-control (Tubbs, 1996) and helps participants connect with their feelings at the forming stage of the group. The need for sensory and tactile awareness is facilitated with particular attention being paid to the hands and their use as the creative tools in the mask making. The form of words and the delivery technique have a significant impact on the subsequent group process. Some images, which for the majority of people promote a sense of calmness, will, for a susceptible few, create anxiety and distraction. Therefore content, tone, volume, pitch and quality of the narration can establish or deter a cordial atmosphere. The facilitator must present this exercise in a relaxed manner to create a soothing ambience. Allied to this is the use of appropriate music, without lyrics, to complement the voice and harmonise the atmosphere. The focus of all these exercises is to bring together the body, the mind and the spirit. The physical surroundings are of importance in sustaining the aesthetic connection. A well-ventilated comfortable space with natural light that allows for freedom of movement is the ideal location for conducting the mask making experience.

Modeling the making of the mask facilitates the development of group norms around issues such as taboo, touch and vulnerability. To acknowledge these requires sensitivity, awareness and understanding the vulnerability implicit in the exposure of the self to the other(s). Here facilitators verbalise potential fears related to safety and trust for group members. This naming of fears and their acceptance at this stage encourages participants to take the risks necessary to engage with the group process.

Facilitators demonstrate the technique using one of themselves as subject or receiver of the mask and the other(s) as the giver of the mask. This exercise can be undertaken by facilitators in pairs or in triads. Triads deliver this process quickly and provide a safer environment for those who may require support at this stage. As this is taking place participants are facilitated to observe and ask questions that may arise for them. This can trigger powerful emotional responses in participants. Facilitators need to be aware of the potential impact that the masking can evoke. For some it creates feelings around the idea of a "death mask," or being smothered or silenced. For others it can provide reassurance that the process is not as threatening as their preconceived notions suggested. The role of facilitation here is to make explicit these issues and allow space for the processing of feelings which arise as well as acknowledging and making the connection with the socio-cultural realities that intersect with the personal and professional lived experience of participants. In our experience this stage has evoked memories of genocide and/or violent death, which prematurely disrupts life's expected rhythm. Successful facilitation is predicated on dealing with the here and now of the experience by participants.

Working Phase

Choosing a Partner

The first task for group members is to choose a partner with whom to work. Making this choice goes to the heart of empowerment where participants have the right to control the events that affect them. We agree with Lee (1994), in that, for the empowerment process to be effective, decision-making must rest with the person and not with the helper. "Empowerment is a reflexive activity, a process capable of being initiated and sustained only by those who seek power or self-determination. Others can only aid and abet this empowerment process" (Simon, 1990, p. 32). In a group where the levels of trust are high, this choice is easier than in a group which is newly formed. For example, the groups with whom we've worked were at very different stages in their formation. This had significant implications for the facilitation of trust in the groups and also affected the value as well as the depth of the experience for participants.

The first group had just come together and were at the beginning stages of formation in the development of safety and trust. Participants on the second programme had been together for nearly a year. Trust levels were high and relationships in the group were strong. Where trust and safety were already established, choosing a partner to work with appeared to be undertaken seamlessly. Members of the first group who were struggling with issues around forming appeared to find this more challenging.

Getting Down and Dirty

Each partnership set decides the order of the mask making process. Following a dialogue between them, one lies prostrate on the floor. The other(s) kneel as they apply the mask making materials. This positioning at ground level is worthy of note, as it is a symbolic representation of the powerlessness and dependency frequently experienced by service users at the hands of social workers. The dynamic duality of the experience of trust and letting go synchronises the momentum that pushes the process forward. In this manner creative energy is released, as participants become involved in the making of the mask. Boundaries are crossed, literally and metaphorically, as they begin to apply the protective Vaseline followed by the gyps which requires them to touch each other's faces. This propels them into a more intimate relationship with the other. There are different reactions among group members to their roles as receiver and giver of the mask. Some are relaxed and happy, enjoying the intimacy which occurs. Others are upset by the exercise and require facilitation to complete the task. In anticipation of the dynamics of power and dependence, facilitators can prepare participants by discussing these issues in advance and thus normalising them.

The receivers can find themselves in an increasingly vulnerable position as they lose the ability for verbal and sensory communication when both the eyes and the mouth are covered by the wet gyps. In order that participants can breathe while the face is covered, the area around the nostrils is left uncovered. Facilitators prepare participants for this isolation by encouraging them to develop advance strategies of non-verbal communication, by which the receiver can indicate anxiety or well being. Examples of this would include hand raising to signal distress or a hand squeeze for well being. The givers can also find themselves challenged by this activity, as it is difficult to prepare for all the responses that can arise. As one participant remarked during the evaluation:

> I was trying to reassure her by using a voice and saying "Are you OK?" when all she wanted me to do was stop and just, you know, just be quiet and be in her own thoughts, and, so I thought I was actually doing something that was relaxing her or making her, you know, feel a little better about things, but actually I wasn't, which was an eye-opener for me.

Birthing

The birthing of the mask, that is when it is taken off the face, is usually an exciting and sacred event. Participants find that the experience connects with deep wellsprings of emotion. For women it has frequent resonance with the life theme and with the births of their children. This emotional response is not only confined to women; men also make the connection to the life theme. New thresholds of awareness lead to new possibilities opening up after the birth of the masks, making a turning point in the development of self and the other. This event may evoke painful memories related to infertility, miscarriage, termination and neo-natal death. Facilitators need to prepare the group for such eventualities and recognise the difficulties that exist for women in discussing these topics, particularly in mixed gender groups. The actual making of the masks facilitates a sense of achievement and of survival, releasing feelings of relief, joy and accomplishment. The energy level in the group is palpable as members seek to share their feelings with each other. Arising from this position of strength, participants may be more able to confront and discuss the impact of painful life experiences. Significantly this energy drives the group to the next stage, which is one of reflection.

Reflections on the Process

Next, participants are requested to reflect upon the process as they experienced it. They engage in a reflective exercise where each individual documents their reactions to the process of giving and receiving. Creative writing affords the opportunity to put words on the experience and move it to a cognitive level. From this process of "moving beyond language and cultural conventions, a new awareness arises of one's own limitations but also of novel avenues of expression and communication" (Luedemann 2003, p. 28). To translate learning from the mask making process it is important to provide questions that scaffold it. The function of the question(s) is to support the learner in their reflective dialogue.

> It is a discussion, which the learner has with him or herself, a kind of reflective soliloquy. In common with a soliloquy we all know that this dialogue with oneself, though seemingly private, is held before an audience. It is not just the content which is important but also the quality of the dialogue as a dialogue. (Doel, Sawdon, & Morrison, 2002, p. 50)

The structure of these questions is critical. They need to be framed clearly and succinctly to guide the learner along the route to connectivity with the universal themes which the mask making excavates. Questions may be constructed that lead learners from description to reflection: from examination of the emotional content of the process to the analysis of wider political forces. The questions focus the learners on what they did, what they felt about the experience and what meaning and understanding they developed from it. Time is allocated specifically for this processing. When completed, the questions are re-configured to discuss the connection between thinking, feeling and behaviour, making links with the personal, cultural and social factors which influence and underpin their understanding.

Once participants have completed their individual reflections they form, first, small and subsequently large groups for voicing and sharing the commonality and diversity of issues that have arisen. Frequently common themes emerge, such as those concerning the life cycle of birth and death, power and dependence, relationships and isolation, giving and receiving.

Painting the Process

The penultimate stage involves each working sub-group joining together to paint the masks. In keeping with the Meitheal principles each person paints the mask of the other. Much dialogue takes place between each set as they revisit their experiences, thus furthering and deepening the process of reflection. As a result new knowledge of *self* and *other* begin to materialise, represented figuratively and graphically by the transformation that takes place by the painting of the mask.

Ending Phase: Creative Dialogue Through Action

The finale involves each participant presenting the mask to the other using the medium of performance. Participants dress the mask for presentation using colourful materials. This is followed by a play of the mask that uses mime, song, dance or words. The finale culminates with the presentation of the mask to each other. Symbolically and literally this actualises the concepts of giving and receiving.

Evaluation

A full group analysis and evaluation is carried out at the end of the workshop. This enables participants to integrate and contextualise their learnings from the mask making experience. It is in this phase that the personal, political and global issues can be revisited and become more explicit. The ongoing tension between text and context can be examined in this forum. People are offered, in addition, the opportunity to reflect upon the total experience and to have a period in which they can wind down and, if necessary, restore the balance of their equilibrium.

Discussion

As educators we are involved in constructing an innovative teaching method which seeks to combine cognition and creativity to tap into the learner's spectrum of abilities (Gardner, 1999). The tension between theory and practice implicit in this duality can be reflective of dichotomies in social work practice. A post-modern critical perspective recognises these dilemmas and seeks to develop ways of knowing which

> constitute(s) an alternative to dominant "logocentric" purely positivistic and empiricist approaches to discovery. With a basis in personal and

concrete experience, it opens the way for marginalised aspects of experience to be incorporated into understandings of the world, for example the emotions and personal history. (Fook, 1999, p. 203)

As groupwork practitioners/facilitators we strive to use the full potential of the group to develop the learner's knowledge, values and skills for strengths-based empowering practice. In operationalising this approach a number of dilemmas have arisen for us.

Structural Issues

Where this method is used in the classroom context certain organisational issues arise, for example, should it be a core or an optional module? To date our practice has been to present it as an option, allowing participants to choose whether they wish to become involved. Another issue is the rigidity of timetabling and the availability of appropriate locations where mask making can be undertaken. Additionally the amount of time available for a workshop determines the format and the quality of the experience. The amount of time needed to develop safety and trust within the group will vary. Maximising the impact of the method is dependent on high levels of trust in the group. To date we have managed to get a group together for a day or two at the most in a very busy curriculum. This has meant limiting ourselves to using mask making as a tool focussing on self in relation to the other, rather than engaging in the other forms that require more time to complete. Ideally we would like a week, in which participants could engage firstly, with the self by making their own mask prior to engaging with the other. At times we find ourselves compromising and in the words of T.S. Eliot "Between the idea and the reality, between the motion and the act, falls the shadow" (Eliot, 1969, p. 85).

Ethical Issues

We are aware that as educators we can be criticised for exposing students and expecting them to expose themselves in activities that may reactivate or reconnect them to painful experiences in their pasts. Our rationale for pursuing this approach rests on the belief that self-awareness is a core competency in social work training. Thus if we are preparing students for social work practice, we must acknowledge and engage with the realities of their previous experiences. It is important that social workers in training have an opportunity to develop awareness of issues concerning intimacy, abuse, ability, gender, power and boundaries for themselves and how these may impact on service users. If we fail to access students to the possibilities implicit in such experiences we must question whether we are best serving their needs or those of service users.

A universal ethical issue concerns the perception of the face as the representation of a person's identity incorporating soul, spirit and essence of the human being. Most cultures both primitive and developed recognise the face as unique. In some primitive cultures taking the person's photograph is feared because it is considered that it steals that individual's spirit. In western cultures new medical technology involving face transplants can encounter the same phenomenon where people show more resistance to donating their faces than other parts of their bodies.

> A face is more than just a physical entity; it is what we communicate with to the world. At the end of the day, only a small number of people will be potential recipients, but what's more interesting is an initial survey showed that while people were open to accepting a face donation, few would be willing to donate. (O'Flaherty, 2002)

Creativity

One of the obstacles that some people encounter is related to their fear of the creative process and their ability to be creative. This is reinforced by fear of the unknown, the need to cross new frontiers. Many practitioners would subscribe to the notion that social work is an art as well as a skill and a discipline. However, their experiences in practice reflect an absence of creative ways of working. By *doing* they discover that creativity is a basic human need. For participants whose training has been dominated by traditional cognitive and behavioural approaches, adapting to a new form of learning is a challenge. Many approach the mask making with a cognitive task-orientated focus in that they want to plan and rationally engage for a predetermined outcome, trying to put a cognitive structure on what is essentially a creative process.

Working with the hands and being led by tactile cues is new and daunting; the expectation of being exposed to aspects of self not yet discovered or deeply buried can strike fear and terror into some people. Breaking down such barriers demands that people take risks and move from "can't do" to something new. In a profession where workers are supposed to be in control of themselves and others this requires them to break the mould and allow the creative dynamic to unfold through the task and reflective dialogue. An additional fear for some concerns the process and their ability to succeed in creating a mask that is sensitively representative of the other. The questions that may arise at this juncture are: "What will happen if I am unable to complete the making of the mask? What if I give up? Can I stop at any point? What will be revealed? Will I be able to cope?" Some of the issues that emerge are connected to participants' inexperience of creative ways of working, their clumsiness in actual handling of materials, their lack of fine motor movements and their inability to see themselves as artists and creators. It is the process of mask making that brings these to consciousness and provides a forum for reflection and theorising.

Transcending Taboos: Heightened Awareness of Self in Relation to the Other

An important life skill is the ability to make relationships with others. This is also a core requirement in the caring professions. However, there is a challenge and a dilemma inherent in the process for the facilitators, with our identified aim being to transcend taboos of touching, proximity and intimacy. Touching the face of another in this context can activate or trigger powerful repressed feelings and memories both positive and negative. The participant experiences the self in relation to the other as part of the process. We are aware that there are greater difficulties involved for some people in the mask making process, for example, survivors of abuse, for men and women working together and for people with different abilities. As one participant remarked on evaluation,

> In terms of the social work practice teaching side or using it as a teaching method, I would suggest that one needs to be really careful about the kind of feelings that it brings up. I just think that it needs to be kept in mind depending on where people are at when they are doing it.

Any memories and traumas that arise for people need to be processed immediately, sometimes at the expense of the task. Active facilitation is the key to staying in touch with the *here and now*, allowing time, enabling members to provide mutual aid in dealing with feelings and issues that have arisen. For us the resolution of this dilemma has been to work as a triad, spreading ourselves among group members and giving ongoing support as required.

Making the Personal Political

The feelings and experiences evoked during mask making are very personal. However the themes that emerge in the reflection and subsequent discussions are universal. In one group for example, the role of women as nurturers, givers and carers led to an analysis of patriarchy. In another group, it awoke memories of the genocide in Rwanda for one participant who had worked in that country. A group discussion of this horrendous event was processed with a focus on understanding the political influences in its genesis. The values and orientation of the facilitators will determine whether or not the global issues are represented in this way. We would always endeavour to facilitate participants to make these connections, but recognise that everyone may not be at this stage. Some members of the group make connections easily; others are more introspective and focus on their own immediate feelings and responses.

Issues of Equality

In the groups that are the subjects of this chapter, we have met resistance in facilitating the inclusion of people with difference. This applies to both gender and ability differences. In relation to gender our experience reflects the predominance of women in social work training in Ireland; consequently, men have found themselves in the minority and on the fringes of the group. Similarly, people with disabilities have experienced equal marginalisation. This has become most evident when choosing a partner with whom to work. We have found that there is a tendency for minority members to be left unchosen and, in order to participate, to need to seek each other out as partners in the process. While recognising members' rights to make their own choices, our dilemma is how we can facilitate the active engagement with difference in the group. This dilemma would not be confined to gender and ability differences but may be present in other forms in other groups.

Results

Democratic Approach to Education

Mask making can be a democratic way of being and doing, giving and receiving. Both mentors and students are engaged equally in the process of how and what is taught and learned. People work together on an equal basis to achieve the task and each person's ability and input is validated. We recognise that there are some people who may not be able to engage easily with the task. To date our experience has been that through discussion of their needs they have been able to participate. This coheres with Habermas's view of an ideal learning activity that enables people to speak openly, honestly, critically allowing dialectical exploration of points of view (Carr & Kemmis, 1986). As an empowering approach, it is the *process* that emerges as the central teaching component. In being governed by the process in this way, we are not always bound to produce a product. The task of mask making is solely a *tool* to achieve learning for understanding. Not completing a mask may offer equal opportunities for learning and awareness development.

Liberating

An anti-oppressive framework recognises the importance of naming differences as a first step to understanding them. These differences include gender, race, age, ability, culture, religion sexual orientation and class. By naming and engaging with these differences from the outset, a culture of liberation can be fostered which is predicated on celebrating and validating difference in partnership with the group. Our experience has demonstrated that this approach can transcend barriers created by language and that working creatively enables the person to experience and view situations in a different way.

Self-actualisation

We have found that mask making has evoked insights that have led to participants reporting increased self-awareness, thus taking the process of self-discovery and self-actualisation a step further. The opportunity to experience a heightened awareness of self in relation to the other is reported by many. For example one participant remarked,

> For me doing the exercise sort of reinforced the thought I had this morning about masks, you know, people are hiding behind masks and yet making a mask is absolutely revealing and you know the whole process really kind of reinforced that.

However, the stage of personal and professional development of participants is a significant factor in terms of outcomes. The depth of engagement and making meaningful connections to where the person comes from and what they bring to the workshop is critical to this process. The level of awareness of self and the other is also important. Our contact with the different groups lead us to believe that those with greater lived and practice experience were brought to a further level of awareness. For the less experienced the production of an artistic product was initially of greater significance than their journey. Their engagement in the process of exploring the unknown where the destination is uncertain but enlightening was at a more gradual rate.

The self-directed nature of the process allows participants to take control over the pace and depth of their learning. The evaluation reflected the diversity of opinion and experiences that the learners took from the mask making process. Many indicated that the day had raised questions about the nature of practice and existence that they needed to examine further.

Finding New Skills and Hidden Talents

For many participants, exposure to the mask-making workshop facilitates them to dig deep within themselves for talents and skills that for much of their lives may have been dormant. The discovery of these talents emerged particularly with the birthing of the mask. These represented both a revelation and actualisation of their creative powers in that abilities and strengths become the focus and are encountered by participants who find validation through knowing that there is something they can do.

Learning about Giving and Receiving

The majority reported increased learning regarding the process of giving and receiving. The following quotation from one of the participants highlights the kind of feedback that we received.

What I found about it was, that it was very good to be on the giving side and the receiving side. This enabled me to know what it is like for a student to be on the receiving side. This is very important when you take a student. We can say that we know the feelings they are having, but we really don't, we just kind of imagine it.

All were very conscious of the power implicit in the student practice teacher relationship. The process provided a context for learning, where dialogue is a central feature in the deconstruction of old beliefs and behaviours and the application of this new found knowledge to practice teaching in social work.

Facilitation

The values and orientation of facilitators will affect the kind and depth of learning attained. As with any group the process does not *just happen* it requires facilitation from the building of trust through the various stages to termination. To gain full value from the process, we believe that the Meitheal approach with its focus on peoples' strengths, co-operation and trans-formation offers a set of principles for empowering practice.

Performance

This penultimate phase of the workshop has much greater potential for development than we have been able to realise to date. Our experience now leads us to believe that more time is required to support the enactment of the performance and to provide for more dynamic and meaningful presentations. This can be achieved by facilitators learning about and employing theatrical skills and increasing the use of mixed media methods. By opening up the performance for further development, we are engaged in a *work in progress* with all the excitement and possibilities that this entails.

Fun

Finally, but not least, it can be an enjoyable and absorbing way to learn. "If we relish what we are doing then it tends to follow that we are more open to learning. If we are enjoying ourselves, learning and knowledge tend to come naturally" (Hickson, 1995, p. xi). Participants can feel good about themselves. The focus is on people's strengths and their pleasure in each other. Fun opens the gates to creativity, transcending barriers and finding new ways of being, doing and learning together.

Conclusion

The contribution to and use of creative means in social work education has not yet received the attention it deserves. "But effective, imaginative, and resourceful problem solving requires more than science. We need to further understand the art side of practice" (Heus & Pincus, 1986, p. 9). It is our belief that good practice in this area involves moving beyond mere cognition to discover the richness and diversity which the lens of creativity reveals. "A post-modern reading prompts us to question everything, but also opens up the possibility of multiple explanations and multiple strategies" (Lane, 1999, in Pease & Fook, 1999, p. 147). Social groupwork using a Meitheal perspective activates and uses the mutual aid component of the group to facilitate this realisation in a more inclusive and integrated approach to education and learning. All social work interventions are predicated on experiences that involve giving and receiving. Mask making is a dynamic tool that can contribute to learning for understanding by actualising the process of giving and receiving in a personal but universally accessible form.

References

Albright, D. (Ed.) (1990). *W. B. Yeats: The poems*, London: J. M. Dent & Son Ltd.

Breton, M. (1995). The potential for social action in groups. *Social Work with Groups*, *18*(2/3), 5–13.

Breton, M. (2002). A rewarding group worker's journey. *Social Work with Groups*, *25*(1–2), 23–29.

Carr, W. and Kemmis, S. (1986). *Becoming critical.* London: Falmer Press.

Cohen, M. and Mullender, A. (Eds.) (2003). *Gender and groupwork*. London and New York: Routledge.

Doel, M. and Sawdon, C. (1999). *The essential groupworker.* London: Jessica Kingsley.

Doel, M. and Sawdon, C., & Morrison, D. (2002) *Learning, practice and assessment: Signposting the portfolio.* London: Jessica Kingsley.

Elias, W., Jones, D., and Normie, G. (Eds.) (1995). Truths without facts: Selected papers from the first three International Conferences on Adult Education and the Arts, Brussels, Belgium: VUB University Press.

Eliot, T. S. (1969). *The complete poems and plays.* London: Faber and Faber

England, Hugh (1983). *Social work as an art.* London: Allen and Unwin.

Fook, J. (1999). Critical reflexivity in education and practice. In B. Pease & and J. Fook (Eds.). *Transforming social work practice* (pp. 195–210). London: Routledge.

Freire, P. (1970) *The pedagogy of the oppressed.* New York: Herder & Herder.

Gardner, H. (1999). *Intelligence reframed.* New York: Basic Books.

Giddens, A. & Reimer, G. (1999). *The politics of postmodernity.* London: Sage Publications.

Gronning, E. and Fougner, A. (2002). How to use your heart as an eye. In D. Jones & G. Normie (Eds.), *Life's rich pattern: Cultural diversity and the education of adults* (pp. 105–114). Boston, Lincs.: SCUTREA & Pilgrim College.

Heus, M. and Pincus, A. (1986). *The creative generalist.* Barnefeld, WI: Micamar Publishing.

Hickson, Andy. (1995). *Creative action methods in groupwork.* Bicester, Oxon.: Winslow Press Ltd.

Kolb, D. (1984) *Experiential learning.* Englewood Cliffs, NJ: Prentice Hall.

Lane, M. (1999). Community development and a postmodernism of resistance. In B. Pease & J. Fook (Eds.). *Transforming social work practice* (pp. 150–160). London: Routledge.

Lee, J. A. B. (1994). *The empowerment approach to social work practice.* New York: Columbia University Press.

Lordan, N. (1996) The use of the sculpt in social groupwork education. *Groupwork,* 9(1), 62–79.

Lordan, N. & Wilson, M. (2002), Groupwork in Europe: Tools to combat social exclusion in a multi-cultural environment. In S. Henry, J. East, & C. Schmitz (Eds.), *Social work with groups: Mining the gold* (pp. 9–30). New York: Haworth Press.

Luedemann, O. (2003). Interacting productively with the familiar and the strange. *Fromm Forum, 7.* Heidelberg: International Eric Fromm Society.

Middleman, R. and Wood, G. G. (1990) *Skills for direct practice in social work.* New York: Columbia University Press.

O' Flaherty, K. (2002). *Irish man to make history with face transplant.* Dublin: Sunday Tribune (12 Jan.).

Pease, B. & Fook, J. (Eds.) (1999). *Transforming social work practice.* London: Routledge.

Powell, F. (1999) New millennium, new social work? *The Irish Social Worker, 17*(3), 13–14.

Schwartz, W. (1971). *The practice of group work.* New York: Columbia University Press.

Simon, B. L. (1990). Rethinking empowerment. *Journal of Progressive Human Services 1*(1), 27–39.

Tubbs, Irene. (1996). *Creative relaxation,* Bicester, Oxon.: Winslow Press.

Wayne, J. & Cohen, C. S. (2001). *Groupwork education in the field.* Alexandria, VA: Council on Social Work Education.

10 Why We Get No Respect

Existential Dilemmas for Group Workers Who Work with Kids' Groups

Andrew Malekoff

Group Workers Who Work with Kids Get No Respect

Group work with kids is rarely neat. It is more abstract than still life, more jazz than classical. Group workers worth their salt invite their young group members to be co-creators. This is a radical concept for many grown-ups, although not a new one. Neither is the antipathy it generates from those within earshot of kids' groups. When one chooses to work with children and youth in groups, skepticism and scorn follow. Group workers can either embrace or avoid the cynics in their midst. What they cannot do is escape them.

One observer, reflecting on group work in the early 1900s said it well:

> group workers were different, often thought of as unprofessional . . . were out of the office more than behind the desk . . . were workers who enjoyed having a meal or party with their people, who used activities like singing and dancing, who weren't neutral but shared their beliefs . . . they were workers whose work appeared chaotic and not so controlled . . . (Middleman & Goldberg, 1992, p. 26)

Even then "the problem of acceptance . . . was felt by many group workers. The scorn exhibited by 'those workers who play with children, run dances, go camping, or teach art and crafts' is well remembered" (Wilson, 1976, p. 25).[1] Attitudes haven't changed over the years. *Group workers who work with kids get no respect.*

We get no respect because our groups make noise and move about, vibrate and explode, laugh and have fun. This does not happen by accident. Yet, at times group workers are ashamed and apologetic. "Sorry, next time I'll try to keep them more quiet . . . I'll try to keep them from making such a mess . . . I'll try to keep them from leaving the room . . ."

If welcoming spontaneity and raw expression is a choice made freely, why apologize? Working with kids in groups generates confusion, misunderstanding, and doubt in colleagues, parents, and relevant others. This is an

---

1   This and the two previous quotes were found in Kurland and Salmon (1998).

inescapable reality for most group workers who work with children and youth. What can we do about it? Three things.

First, we must value, cherish, and publicly celebrate what we do, encouraging others to stay the course. *Second*, we must become itinerant educators who travel the land demystifying what we do and what happens in kids' groups. *Third*, to do this work, and to do it well, we need to take care of ourselves.

Group Work with Kids is a Beautiful Thing

What Does it Feel Like to Work with Kids in Groups?

Group work with kids is

> like a roller coaster ride, but in a new configuration each time around; harrowing yet fun, with unexpected twists and turns, ascents and declines; you experience anxious anticipation and vertigo-inducing surround-sound; you wish it would never end, and you hope it never does. Sometimes, however, it's not so exciting—more like a crawling commute in rush hour traffic, enervating, meandering, puzzling, endless. (Malekoff, 1997, p. vii)

Group work with kids is a half-eaten slice of pizza, a shirt hanging out, a chair leaning back, a runny nose, mismatched socks, and a dripping ice cream cone. At times it can also be compared to a sunset. *Group work with kids is a* beautiful *thing*.

The road for group workers who work with kids is clogged with those who insist that the only worthwhile group is one that speaks politely and insightfully. Arch-enemies of the noise police, group workers who work with kids tend to be viewed as amateurs dabbling where deeper, more learned, and more individualized work is necessary.

Our work often looks like it just crawled out of bed. Whatever it means to be politically correct in the human services, we're not. At our best what we are is a legion of Detective Columbos, rumpled and befuddled yet dogged and savvy. We often mirror our groups. As some might say, "He or she is a real piece of work." This may or may not come through in outward appearance, but almost always comes through in a group worker's spirit.

Group Work with Kids is Filled with Good Stories

It is rare that practitioners working with individuals, families or groups of adults face serial scrutiny about their work. Group workers who work with children and youth in groups are consistently confronted with raised eyebrows and interrogations that all add up to one question, "What is going on in there?" (The complete poem is contained in the appendix.)

We bring our kids to you,
To see what you can do;

They meet a bunch of others,
See, we are all their mothers;

We hear a lot of noise,
And, yes, boys will be boys (and girls will be girls);

But what is going on in there?,
Nothing much we fear (Malekoff, 1997, pp. 50–52)

Group workers who work with kids must become educators, itinerant teachers who demystify group work. Choosing to practice group work with kids assumes a need to educate others about what one does. Being defensive may be a natural impulse, but is not an option.

How do we educate and demystify group work? Beyond scholarship and formal presentation, which are not for everyone, stories and poetry are a start. Storytelling is less daunting than scholarly writing and lecturing. Everyone can do it. All group workers tell stories about their groups. Sometimes they're war stories and sometimes they're sweet stories. Either way, group work with kids is filled with good stories. And every story has a lesson.

How to get started? Write a story down, think about what lesson it tells and presto, you have an illustration and an accompanying concept. I keep a file of stories. Most of them are less than one page. I give each of them a title. One of my favorite stories is called "The Photo" and it goes like this:

> It was an early meeting of the "changing family group," composed of 9-, 10-, and 11-year-old boys and girls. Each of the members had experienced some upheaval in their families. Their parents had divorced and separated, and in some cases a parent had died. The homework assignment given at the end of this particular meeting was for them to bring something to the next meeting that was meaningful to them. Allie, a 9-year-old whose father had died just months before said, "I know what I'd like to bring but I'd have to dig him up." And then unexpectedly Jimmy, the most physically active and distractible member of the group who was by then all over the room and into the toys and games on the shelves, stopped what he was doing. He bounded over to Allie and got about as physically close to her as he could, without touching her. And then without asking what she meant by her statement, Jimmy whispered to her, "You could bring a picture." After a moment, Allie reached into her pink plastic purse and remove a tattered photograph. Her action spurred the others to move towards her and form a semi-circle around her so that each could get a good look at the snapshot she held of her smiling father.

Great stories like "The Photo" help to celebrate and demystify group work with kids. They elevate the work and demonstrate its elegance. I use this story to teach about group workers sharing authority with group members, what mutual aid looks like, tapping into group members' strengths, and inviting the whole person to participate. And whenever I tell the story, no matter how often I do, it gives me goose bumps and makes me feel good.

Poetry is another way to celebrate and demystify the work. Why poetry? Poetry is a universal translator. It allows me some catharsis and a shorthand way to play with the feelings and concepts that underpin the work. After all, I have always felt that group work with kids is *poetry in motion*. Or, as I have argued, *all that jazz*. Like a great jam session some of our best work comes when we throw away the sheet music, not an easy choice if traveling in a curriculum-driven landscape. Poetry is one way to capture the power and magic of group work.

My Kind of Group Work (GW)

- It's the GW with ragged edges that belie its genius.
- It's the GW that can be messy and noisy and chaotic and profound, all at once.
- It's the GW where children and youth are *group members,* not *clients* or *patients.*
- It's the GW where the group worker does *with* the group, not *for* or *to* the group.
- It's the GW where *learning by doing* is as important as *insight by talking.*
- It's the GW that is not ashamed to laugh and have fun.
- It's the GW that makes use of everyday life and not only programmed activities and canned curricula.
- It's the GW where responsibility is shared by worker and group members.
- It's the GW that threatens grown ups who are uptight.
- It's the GW that welcomes parents, and doesn't avoid them.
- It's the GW that invites the rational *and* the spontaneous.
- It's the GW that lets difficult, painful, and taboo subjects see the light of day.
- It's the GW that begins with need, not a label and diagnosis.
- It's the GW that respects pathology, but never worships it.
- It's the GW that embraces strengths, not deficits.
- It's the GW that invites the whole person to participate, not just the troubled, broken, and hurt parts.
- It's the GW that has a social conscience.
- It is the GW with a dual focus of individual change *and* social reform.
- It's the GW that schools of social work once held close, and then abandoned.
- It's the GW that is a rare gem in the human services, yet faces extinction.
- It's the GW that *is* the hidden treasure in youth development.

- It's the GW that needs workers to stay the course, administrators to support the way, and missionaries to spread the word. (Malekoff, 2002, p. 29)

If you care to explain what you are doing you need to deconstruct practice. So try to take it apart through poetry, narrative, or music. It is a good discipline. It is a process that allows us to celebrate and educate and integrate at the same time.

How Do We Take Care of Ourselves?[2]

Conferences like this weekend's offer participants fellowship and support—a place to connect. A good conference should also offer useful concepts, good ideas, practical skills, and a clear vision. I always feel that if I can leave a conference with one or two good ideas or concepts or skills; perhaps a connection with someone I never met before; and maybe a little inspiration, validation, and vision: then I'm way ahead of the game. I also look for a lift, something to charge my batteries to help me to hang in there with the difficult work ahead, in this most difficult time that we live in.

In this spirit, I'd like to leave you with a meditation to take back to your workplaces, and I'll end with a poem I wrote that has become a kind of group work anthem for me. The meditation reminds me to find a circle of colleagues I can count on.

First, the meditation. It's about *how we take care of ourselves and how important it is to have the support of colleagues.* If you work with kids in groups, you *do* need to take care of yourself. But how?

How do we take care of ourselves? When you've finished a particularly difficult group meeting that left you reeling and dazed, what helps? Or what about a meeting in which you are left feeling deeply moved and you know you have just been a part of something special? Is your colleague in the next room or down the hall or a phone call away someone whom you are eager to see and share with? Or do you flinch at the thought? Does the place in which you spend the better part of your day, and maybe evening, invite collegial support? *How do we take care of ourselves?*

What we know about groups is relevant here. *First,* we know that people are social beings who need the affirmation and support of others. *Second,* we know that a good group is one where members can really be themselves and be accepted by the other group members, that in a good group there is no need to put on airs or to pretend to be someone one is not in order to gain the acceptance of one's peers. *Third,* we know that in a group attention must be paid simultaneously to the total group *and* to each of the individual group members.

---

2   This section is adapted from Malekoff and Kurland (1995).

How do we take care of ourselves? Such basic principles apply. We all need affirmation, support, and understanding from at least some of our colleagues. We need to be able to be ourselves with those colleagues and to know that they will accept us, even when we may disagree about particular approaches or points of view.

And, of course, there are times when we are nourished by solitude, when we take the time to think things through on our own. Such moments can generate creative expression, expression for no reason but to satisfy one's soul. Music, art, writing, or whatever activities we use to tap the spirit in our groups can work for us as individual youth workers as well. Such moments of solitude are valued, especially when one is solid in the knowledge that one also "belongs" to a "good group" of colleagues.

True colleagues are, indeed, rare. We need them. We need to seek them out. And when we find them, we need to treasure them. And in the work that we do, that is so very demanding, difficult, moving, and special, we also need to be real colleagues to others.

Appendix

What is Going on in There?: Question and Response[3]

What is going on in There? (The Question)

> We bring our kids to you,
> To see what you can do;
>
> They meet a bunch of others,
> See, we are all their mothers;
>
> We hear a lot of noise,
> And, yes, boys will be boys (and girls will be girls);
>
> But what is going on in there?,
> Nothing much we fear.
>
> Our rooms are side by side,
> And it's not my style to chide;
>
> But your group's a bit too crazy,
> And what you're doing's kind of hazy;
>
> After all they're here to talk,
> Yet all they do is squeal and squawk;

---

3 This poem appears in Andrew Malekoff (1997). *Group Work with Adolescents: Principles and Practice*. New York: The Guilford Press, pp. 50–52.

What it going on in there?
Nothing much we fear.

Hi I'm from the school,
And it's not my style to duel;

But Johnny's in your group,
And I know that you're no dupe;

But his dad has called on me,
to gain some clarity;

So what is going on in there?,
Nothing much, I fear.

Now here we are alas,
Facing you en masse;

We haven't got all day,
So what have you to say;

About this thing called group,
This strange and foggy soup;

Just what is going on in there?,
Nothing much, we fear.

What is Going on in There? (The Response)

If you
really
wish to
know,
have a
seat,
don't plan
to go.
It will
take
awhile
to get,
but you
will
get it,
so
don't you
fret.

A group
begins
by building
trust,
chipping away
at the
surface crust.

Once
the uneasy
feeling is
lost,
a battle rages
for who's
the boss;
Kings and
Queens
of what's
okay
and who
shall
have the
final say.

Once that's
clear
a moment
of calm,
is quickly
followed
by the
slapping of
palms.

A clan
like feeling
fills
the air,
the
sharing
of
joy,
hope,
and
despair.

Family
dramas
are replayed,
so new
directions
can be
made.

Then in
a while
each
one
stands out,
confident
of his
own
special
clout.

By then
the group
has
discovered
its
pace,
a secret gathering
in a
special place.

Nothing
like it
has occurred
before,
a bond
that exists
beyond
the door.

And
finally
it's time
to say
good-bye,
a giggle,
a
tear,

a
hug,
a
sigh.

Hard to
accept,
easy to
deny,
the
group
is
gone
yet
forever
alive.

So you've
asked me
"what is
going
on in
there?,"
I hope
that my
story has
helped
make it
clear.

Maybe
now
it is
easier
to see,
that a
group
has a
life,
just
like
you
and
like
me.

References

Kurland, R. & Salmon, R. (1998). *Teaching a methods course in social work with groups*. Alexandria, VA: CSWE.

Malekoff, A. (1997). *Group work with adolescents: Principles and practice*. New York: The Guilford Press.

Malekoff, A. (2002). My kind of group work, *The New Social Worker, 9*(3), 29.

Malekoff, A. & Kurland, R. (1995). Editorial. *Social Work with Groups, 18*(5), 1–2.

Middleman, R. & Goldberg, G. (1992). Group work and the Heimlich Maneuver: Unchoking social work education. In D. F. Fike & B. Rittner (Eds.), *Working from strengths: The essence of group work* (pp. 16–39). Miami, FL: Center for Group Work Studies.

Wilson, G. (1976). From practice to theory: A personalized history. In R. W. Roberts & H. Northen (Eds.), *Theories of social work with groups* (pp. 1–44). New York: Columbia University Press.

11 Traumatic Grief Groups for Children, Adolescents and their Caregivers

A Short-Term Treatment Model[1,2]

Helen B. Mullin and Deborah S. Langosch

The death of a significant family member has long been recognized as a major stressor on a family, especially when the deceased is a child's primary caregiver. Krupnick and Solomon (1987, as cited in Piper, McCallum, & Azim, 1992) suggest that the risk factors for future development of pathological grief are the death of a parent, or significant caregiver, before a child reaches the age of five; during early adolescence for boys whose fathers die; or for girls under age eleven whose mothers die. The Jewish Board of Family and Children's Services' (JBFCS) Loss and Bereavement (L&B) group model (Schilling, Koh, Abramovitz, & Gilbert, 1992; Schoeman & Kreitzman, 1997) was first implemented in 1987. The outcomes for families treated in this model suggest that children do experience the death of their significant caregiver(s) as a traumatic event.

The experiences of many families exposed to traumatic death such as 9/11 and other psychologically assaultive deaths call for special attention to the impact of trauma on all family members. The treatment protocol needs to address both trauma and grief.

Unless there are attempts to address the family's level of traumatic stress, the grief work rarely occurs. This chapter builds on the theoretical basis of our L&B model combined with the fast-growing trauma recovery theories (Fleming & Robinson, 2002). It will describe the enhancement of the L&B model and the experience of facilitating Traumatic Grief (TG) groups for children and their caregivers.

Trauma and traumatic grief have been discussed thoroughly elsewhere (Jacobs, 1999; Prigerson & Jacobs, 2002; Russell, 1998). Trauma is defined as any injury which renders someone helpless and powerless. The traumatic

1   Special acknowledgement given to all of the Loss and Bereavement Supervisory Team who helped in the supervisory and consultative aspects of these groups as they have evolved: Robert Abramovitz, MD; C.V. Koh, MD; Hillel Hirshbein, LCSW, MPH; Ruth Kreitzman, LCSW; Linda Payne, LCSW; Len Pilaro, Ph.D.; Phyllis Schimel, LCSW; and in memoriam, Linda Schoeman, Ph.D.
2   Grateful acknowledgements to Michael L. Black, Ph.D. and Mary R. Pagurelias for their assistance in the final preparation of this manuscript.

injury may be biological, spiritual, emotional, psychological, or situational and treatment will need to address each arena. The injury may be seen and objectively traumatic or unseen and subjectively traumatic.

Traumatic grief is a separation-distress related disorder which occurs after the death of a significant other with symptoms of being devastated and traumatized by death. The symptomatic disturbance causes clinically significant impairment in social, occupational, or other important areas of functioning. The use of "traumatic" in the name of the disorder describes the phenomenology rather than the etiology (Jacobs, 1999).

Grief Reactions of Children and Adolescents

Children's and adolescents' ability to grieve and their grief reactions have been widely documented (Webb, 1993; Worden, 1996). The grief work is done in pediatric doses and over an extended period of time (Koh, 2000). At each developmental juncture, the meaning of the loss is renegotiated. Children's successful coping with the traumatic materials and grief is determined by the child's:

(a) access to supportive adult caregivers who provide for basic human needs for safety and survival,
(b) pre-morbid level of functioning,
(c) developmental understandings of death,
(d) the internal or external levels of the trauma, and
(e) caregivers' ability to cope with the intensity of the trauma (Goodman, 2002a).

Grieving families seek mental health services for their children because some of the maladaptive grief reactions interfere with family functioning. Symptomatically, children may be more aggressive, more belligerent, or conversely, more withdrawn. Children under the age of seven can be told of a death and minutes later be playing happily. It may appear that they are not grieving; however, they need to approach and avoid the death due to its overwhelming nature. They may also exhibit regressive behaviors as a response to parental death. When coping with death, children can also exhibit considerable resiliency (Trad & Greenblatt, 1990).

Latency-aged children may exhibit heightened anxiety or increased worry about the well-being of the surviving caregivers. Depending on the nature of the death, some children may somaticize symptoms similar to the illness of the deceased. Often they believe that they are responsible for the death, yet unable to share these concerns. While most children have a decline in school performance, sometimes their reaction to the death improves academics as the "intellectualization" becomes a defense against the trauma and/or grief reactions.

When confronted with a caregiver's death, adolescents are more prone to depressive and/or aggressive symptoms (Noppe & Noppe, 1996). The effects of trauma and grief as experienced by teens may create a sense of finality in their world, challenge their developmental sense of infallibility, and complicate the developmental separation-individuation stages of adolescence.

The Original Loss and Bereavement Model

Twelve consecutive sessions are held in the L&B model and these are loosely divided into three phases: a beginning, middle, and end. Group cohesion is built during the beginning phase where rules are established, the group names itself, and participants begin to tell parts of their stories. Symbolic expressive therapies such as creative arts are utilized and continue throughout the group. They provide a constructive and safe outlet for the expression of feelings in a displaced form and are especially advantageous for work with non-verbal and young children. They also serve as vehicles for talking about the aspects of death and the children's grief reactions (Goodman, 2002a; Goodman, 2002b; Spring, 1994; Webb, 1993).

The tools for the middle phase include creating symbolic representations of the child's relationship with the deceased caregiver by making a memory book of the deceased or a photo album that tells the story of their lives together. In these exercises it is important that the therapists encourage the children to share what they have created without pressuring them. Often one child's writing or drawing generates a therapeutic and helpful discussion that relates to the whole group's concerns and feelings.

For adolescents, it is essential that therapists utilize age-appropriate contemporary media (see Appendix B). Some of the current rap and hip-hop artists reflect the adolescents' internal, affective response to the world. Music and music videos that are expressions of their feelings act as a buffer to the traumatic materials since discussing lyrics is less uncomfortable and less embarrassing than talking about one's own emotions. However, the work of the therapists must be to connect the medium to the teen's internal expressions. Teens are asked to keep a journal to record their reactions and progress, as well as personal thoughts and feelings, and then report back to the group.

The end phase helps bring closure to the group process. The task of this part of the group embodies Worden's (1996) fourth stage of grief: a relocation of the deceased in memory. In combined groups, children and caregivers share mementos of the deceased. They may also have a question and answer session to help increase the family communication and begin to look at their future lives together without the deceased.

Conjointly run groups for both the bereaved child and the surviving caregiver(s) are integral to this model, thus caregiver participation in the caregivers group is a requisite for a child's participation in the children's group. The children need to know there is a caregiver who cares enough about them to participate in the companion group. Without this participation, younger teens experience a sense of abandonment when the affective-laden part of the group is encountered, while older teens may not need to have a companion caregiver group. The goal of the caregivers' group is twofold: first, they must address their own grief issues and second, be able to talk with the child about the death experience. Both caregivers' and children's groups are psycho-educational, and clinical short-term focused groups. Schoeman and Kreitzman (1997) offer a full description of the tasks and clinical processes of the caregivers' group. Schilling et al. (1992) fully outline those for the children's groups.

The caregivers' group is led by one therapist while two therapists lead the children's group. This allows for greater attention to each child's needs, as ways to process and cope with the loss are learned. Two therapists in a potentially emotion-laden group help decrease the risk of secondary traumatization for the therapists (Bloom, 2002). While the groups are being formed and facilitated, all the therapists involved participate in a weekly supervisory session. At the termination of the group, the supervisory sessions also assess future treatment needs for the participants.

Children are grouped by developmental ages and sibling pairs are included if indicated. Exclusion criteria for participants are an existing psychosis, active suicidal ideation, or a child's apparent inability to be emotionally related to others.

The L&B model addresses many behavioral components of children's and adolescents' grief reactions (Schilling et al., 1992; Schoeman & Kreitzman, 1997) and it forms the structure for the grief work done in the TG model. Both models incorporate Worden's (1991, 1996) four, non-sequential tasks of mourning:

(a) accept the reality of the loss,
(b) feel the full range of emotions about the loss,
(c) adjust to an environment in which the deceased is missing, and
(d) shift from an actual relationship with the deceased to a symbolic one.

The Traumatic Grief (TG) Group Model

The TG model incorporates all of the processes of the L&B model described above and includes additional activities that are specifically geared to the traumatic aspect of the death. Following a traumatic event, most symptoms fall into three categories:

(a) re-experiencing the event with intrusive memories triggered by sights, sounds, etc.;
(b) hyper-arousal with an anxious, irritable, and erratic emotional state; and
(c) avoidance and numbing of responsiveness so as not to be overwhelmed by feelings of powerlessness and helplessness (Ehrenreich, 2001; Saltzman, Pynoos, Steinberg, Aisenburg, & Layne., 2001; Stubenbort, Donnelly, & Cohen, 2001; van der Kolk, 1996).

Trauma recovery treatment protocols (Cohen, Stubenbort, Greenberg, Padlo, Shipley, Mannarino, & Deblinger, 2001; Layne, Saltzman, & Pynoos, 2002) address these symptoms by increasing coping mechanisms that ultimately allow for a healthy, uncomplicated bereavement process.

Special Considerations Engaging Caregivers

In early contact with traumatically bereaved families, special care is taken with caregivers. Issues associated with their traumatic experience often need to be assessed before group treatment is offered. One such issue is the caregivers' avoidance of their own traumatization, insisting "I am just here for the children," thus denying their own trauma and grief issues (Ehrenreich, 2001; Goodman, 2002b). While this dynamic is also true of the L&B model, TG caregivers are often more fragile, vulnerable, fearful, and more protective of their children, making the group more precarious that the original L&B caregivers' group.

A caregiver's ability to cope with the intensity of the trauma is a major factor in the potential recovery for a child (Goodman, 2002a). Caregivers will say, "If I can hold it together, then my child won't be hurt anymore." What really occurs is the caregiver may project his/her denied needs and anxieties onto the child. The myth that treatment will re-traumatize the child needs to be addressed to prevent a premature termination of the family's participation, as will the myth that "needing help = weakness." Traumatized caregivers need assurance that they and their children can tolerate the group process. It is helpful to meet with the caregiver several times before engaging the children. These early interventions in the screening process create safety for a traumatized family as it is engaged.

Trauma Recovery Techniques

All of the trauma recovery techniques serve to

(a) create safety,
(b) help develop effective coping skills which increase affect competence,
(c) provide opportunities to progress through the traumatic materials from a Gradual Exposure (GE) to a comprehensive narrative, and
(d) when possible, begin the grief work.

The GE is essentially the working-through phase for the traumatic aspects to the loss. Coping skills aid in maintaining a balance between the containment of overwhelming feelings or behaviors and the expression of the emotionality related to the death.

Creating safety is a concept comparable to any beginning group but with greater emphasis than the L&B model. In the TG group, the therapists build safety by helping the members connect. The creation of a personal safety plan is also critical in order to respond to the question "What if I get too overwhelmed?" As the group develops a list of responses, stress reduction and relaxation skills are taught and creative arts may be used. Initially, the therapists limit disclosure of the traumatic material. They interpret, identify, and name the behaviors and their related feelings as they are associated with traumatic grief. This begins the education about feelings that are refined as the group progresses. Psycho-education about trauma and teaching coping and relaxation skills increases a sense of safety within the group. In the post-9/11 world of adolescent cynicism that challenges the idea of anything being safe, safety is emphasized as a "here and now" experience of what will happen in the room.

Affect competence is built by helping participants identify their own feelings and the impact of those feelings. Affect competence broadens the notion of "affect tolerance" (Russell, 1998) by including the ability to

(a) effectively de-somaticize one's emotional experience,
(b) identify emotions as theirs or as part of one's subjective experience,
(c) sustain attention to one's feelings without being overwhelmed by them, and
(d) use them to form new attachments to others (Pilaro, 2002).

Building affect competence includes use of expressive and artistic therapies combined with cognitive behavioral interventions that help to connect thought, feelings, and behaviors.

Additional TG techniques include relaxation and coping skills, feeling identification exercises with a mixture of Cognitive Behavioral Therapies (CBT), expressive therapies, and exposure therapies. These interventions allow for a GE to the traumatic material and prepares for a telling of the traumatic narrative. The time spent on each skill is fluid as it is both a sequential and circular process. The time determinants are the feelings and actions of the children and their ability to tolerate more of their narratives. Once a safety or coping skill is taught, it continues to be utilized and refined as the group progresses.

Relaxation Techniques

Stress Inoculation Techniques (SIT) (Cohen et al., 2001) are used throughout the group work to contain flooding and anxiety and to control affective responses to potentially traumatic material. Relaxation techniques focus participants on activities that self-soothe. For example, participants are taught deep-breathing exercises and progressive muscle relaxation. In the latter, the children are shown how to tense and relax specific muscle groups. The accompanying image of a wet piece of spaghetti or a limp Raggedy Ann or Andy may help a child visualize these exercises (Cohen et al., 2001). Adolescents often need a creative focus, like imagining a previously safe place in a relaxation or meditation practice session to minimize interference from inappropriate thoughts and feelings.

Thought-stopping techniques are used to help all participants develop greater control over intrusive, repetitive, painful memories, feelings, or thoughts. For example, saying "go away," substituting a calmer mental image, or snapping a rubber band may be statements or actions that replace an unwanted thought with a welcome one. A scale of 1 to 10 to measure levels of disturbance or anxiety can be used here. Sometimes, children want to hold onto their belief that thoughts and feelings are out of their control. While these techniques are taught and learned, often small parts of the traumatic story are told. The groups begin the gradual exposure to the traumatic material, while learning the skill.

Affective Competence Exercises

Any activity that helps participants name and own their feelings would qualify for this type of exercise. Bibliotherapy (reading a book on trauma or loss), showing a movie, and/or listening to a CD are some less direct ways to have discussions about feelings and the beginning of feeling identification. Using pictures of situations and creating a story based on facial expressions also help with feeling recognition.

An easy technique for younger children is a "feeling basket." The basket contains several strips of paper on which is written a feeling word. The children read the feeling word and then act it out. This charade-like exercise can be adapted to adolescents, by assigning a body part, e.g., hands, feet, face, mouth, etc. with which to enact the charade. Care must be taken in the choosing of the body part, e.g., you may get unwanted gestures matching anger with fingers.

Throughout all of these exercises, therapists monitor affective response, listen for any cognitive distortions, and answer any questions about trauma or grief that arise. Therapists also offer validation and normalization of the feelings and thoughts that surface in this and later stages of the group. If a child begins to feel anxious, upset, fearful, etc., the therapist reminds the participant to utilize the learned SIT techniques as actions to take.

Expressive Therapy Techniques

Activities that are used to create safety and affect competence may also include:

(a) drawing a picture of the family both before and after the traumatic loss,
(b) having puppets enact or tell the traumatic story,
(c) individual or group painting and drawing,
(d) reading a book (see Appendix A) or writing about death,
(e) creating clay representations of the death, trauma, funeral, etc.,

(f) creating a collage where the fragmented pieces make a whole picture
     (symbolic of the integration needed for resolving trauma), or
(g) using a collage to represent their affective response to the trauma.

Suggestions for contemporary music and videos are included in Appendix
B. Before using any of these items, the content should be reviewed as well as
the music video attached to a song, as both are the images that teens will have
with the music.

The feeling mandala is an art therapy technique that is useful with all age
groups. It is a drawing activity that teens do not experience as infantilizing.
In this three-part exercise the group is asked to identify a list of feelings to
describe their traumatic losses. Then, as a group they attribute a color to each
of them, e.g., yellow = sadness, red = anger, blue = depression. For young
children it is best to limit the number of feelings to five or six. For older teens
and adults, one might consider ranking the many feelings articulated to the
top six to eight feelings. All members are given a piece of paper with a large
blank circle on it (the mandala) and asked to color it in using the colors they
identified to answer one of the following questions: What are your feelings
about the death? What are your feelings about yourself right now? How do
you feel about the person who died? What is the impact of the trauma right
now? A case example of this technique follows:

> T., a 17-year-old Hispanic teenager, attended an eight-week trauma and
> loss group at his high school. Initially, he was quiet and remote. He
> appeared angry and did not initiate discussions. When asked, he said that
> he had experienced the death of a close friend's mother as a result of the
> 9/11 tragedy. Fragments of this event emerged slowly and were not
> organized. Early in the group he wrote: "Distance and solitude gives me
> protection in order to survive life."
>
> The mandala exercise seemed to be a pivotal turning point in the group
> for him. T. drew the Chinese ying/yang symbol, and his colors represented
> pain, depression, and sorrow. Typically, the ying/yang connotes balance
> and the two sides are symmetrical and reversals of one another. However,
> T.'s ying/yang was not a reversal. He described how he wished for more
> balance and calm in his life, instead of all the pain and sadness he felt.
>
> Following this, T. shared with the group that his two best friends'
> mothers had died as a result of the WTC disaster—one was burned in the
> fire, lived for several weeks, and then died. The other friend's mother had
> a heart attack shortly after the death of the first friend's mother. Because
> both of these women had been like aunts to him, T. was coping with
> profound sorrow and anger.
>
> Towards the end of the group, T. discovered boxing, his father's
> profession. T. began to talk about how boxing allowed him both to
> control and vent his rage without getting in trouble. He also shared his
> pride in his father's accomplishments and his own aspirations to succeed.

Clearly, this experience for T. could only be a beginning, but the hope was that he could continue to benefit from the tools he learned during the group.

Cognitive and Behavior-Focused Skills

As part of the process of understanding one's feelings, age-appropriate CBT techniques are used. One of these skills demonstrates the links between feelings, behaviors and thoughts (Beck, 1995; Cohen et al., 2001; Follette, Ruzek, & Abueg, 1998; O'Donohue, Fanetti, & Elliott, 1998). The model used by Cohen et al. (2001) has a cognitive triangle designed with thoughts, feelings, and behaviors at each point of the triangle. Children are helped to understand the differences and relationships among the three components. If they can see how the three are interrelated (feelings are in response to thoughts which can lead to actions), they can learn to constructively change all three. Hurtful thoughts, such as ones relating to self-criticism, distrust, feeling unloved or unwanted, hopelessness, helplessness, and self-blame, can be replaced with helpful or hopeful thoughts which can lead to a changed perception and contribute to a more adaptive response.

The adolescent variation comes from the work of UCLA's Trauma Center (Layne et al., 2002). Built on the more developed cognitive processes of teens, the cognitive pyramid shows the relationship among situations, thoughts, and feelings. In this triangle, the situation represents what is happening outside, the thoughts represent what is happening inside, and the feelings are just that, feelings. The task for adolescents is to learn that thought distortions (inside of themselves) are intimately connected to their feelings. Therefore, changing the thought may change the feelings; thus, the teen may respond more adaptively to a situation.

In each of these techniques practicing the learned skills is encouraged. The process of acquiring the knowledge and awareness of this interrelational dynamic is based on the repetitive application of the skills. These techniques become the safety tools that the child or teen utilizes in the next phase of the TG group. Caregivers have been helped by these same CBT and self-soothing techniques.

Trauma-Focused Techniques

As the skills are developed, participants learn to name and express what they are feeling and to manage their emotional flooding and intrusive thoughts or images. They have learned to recognize the link between their thoughts and their feelings. In this skill development gradual exposure to the traumatic material is taking place. The therapists, for their part, have been noting all that may interfere with the full integration of the traumatic materials associated with the death of the caregiver.

The unifying technique that addresses the traumatic experience and allows for the working through of the traumatic material is the recitation of the comprehensive narrative. The goal of GE is to develop a means of coping with traumatic reminders and to decrease feeling overwhelmed and flooded by the intensity of affective responses (Cohen et al., 2001; Saltzman et al., 2001).

Over several sessions, children/teens are encouraged to describe more and more details of what happened before, during, and after the trauma/death, as well as accompanying thoughts and feelings during these times (Layne et al., 2002). Because anxiety may increase during the telling of the story, the therapist monitors the intensity of the feelings and suggests CBT techniques to help contain flooding. The goal is to build a narrative that is experienced as less traumatizing.

The therapist's role is to validate the child's experience. The therapists should be especially attentive to issues related to self-blame, guilt, shame, helplessness, and rage. If a child is emoting more or becoming anxious, then asking for factual information (which helps the child think rather than feel) is recommended. The movement through the narrative is the most important aspect of the work. The most intensive part of this comprehensive narrative is confronting the thought distortions that may be keeping the child/teen stuck. This process often elucidates the fantasies the children may have, e.g., the "coulda, woulda, and shoulda" that are part of the trauma and grief recovery work distortions. With these distortions, CBT skills are applied in order to create a more adaptive thought. As each exposure sessions ends, the therapists must help reinforce the child's adaptive defenses, so that the child and group do not leave feeling too vulnerable. This is actually why the children's groups generally end with a shared snack and a calming period, which allows for a reconstitution of their coping egos.

Once the group process has allowed for the de-sensitizing and integration of the traumatic death, the group then follows the integrating aspects of the traumatic grief as has been described in the L&B model. At this juncture, the group can tolerate the intensive grief reactions that will follow. This allows for the integration of the "good, the bad, and the ugly" of the deceased, and an integration of one's identity apart from the deceased. The final sessions of the TG group, like the L&B group, move the participants back into the world. There is a strong opportunity to re-establish the expected developmental markers. At the end of the caregivers' group, we remind them that the child or teen will need to renegotiate the meaning of this loss at each developmental juncture.

Evaluation

Although there has not been a formal evaluation process to determine the efficacy of the TG group model, there has been anecdotal evidence that strongly supports the value of this approach. Most children and caregivers reported a reduction of symptoms. They have shared that using the CBT techniques provided them considerable relief. When the therapists compare children's drawings and writings from the beginning to those at the end of the group, they have observed positive changes. There is more substance to their narrative and the artwork is richer and broader in its expression of feelings. In the final family exit interview, caregivers and children alike report better communication around the trauma and death, and greater understanding between them.

Conclusion

This chapter presented the enhancement of the well-established L&B model to accommodate and respond to families that have had significant traumatic losses. The work presented is an eclectic composition of some of the prevailing treatment approaches. It is a model that addresses the symptom picture of trauma by teaching skills that specifically have been shown to counteract the impact of trauma. The essential part of the traumatic grief work may well be the development of the trauma narrative. Within this part of the group, the worst fear or the most numbing thought distortion surfaces and is addressed. The grief and trauma work may alleviate guilt, self-blame, and/or distortion. The caregiver's role in clarifying family secrets and correcting misinformation becomes a significant healing process for the entire family.

The events of September 11th catapulted the mental health profession into a trauma-recovery frame. Special care is taken in the supervisory sessions to process the effects of secondary traumatization. Although outcome studies may well be a needed next step, for now, the L&B and TG clinicians are "in the trenches" providing sound, clinically based treatment models for dealing with traumatically bereaved children and their caregivers. The nature of the work yet ahead will be to apply what is being learned in the 9/11 recovery efforts of our communities devastated by violence and traumatic deaths.

References

Beck, J. S. (1995). *Cognitive therapy: Basics and beyond*. New York: Guilford Press.

Bloom, S. (2002). *Effects of secondary traumatization*. Unpublished presentation at Jewish Board of Family and Children's Services Interdivisional Lecture series, September 25, 2002.

Cohen, J., Stubenbort, K., Greenberg, T., Padlo, S., Shipley, C., Mannarino, A. P., & Deblinger, E. (2001). *Cognitive behavioral therapy for traumatic bereavement in children: Group treatment manual*. Pittsburgh, PA: Center for Traumatic Stress in Children and Adolescents, Department of Psychiatry, Allegheny General Hospital.

Ehrenreich, J. H. (2001). *Coping with disasters: A guide to psychosocial intervention* (revised ed.). Available at http://www.mhwwb.org.

Fleming, S. & Robinson, P. (2002). Grief and cognitive-behavioral therapy: The reconstruction of meaning. In M. S. Stroebe, R. O. Hannsson, W. Stroebe, & H. Schut (Eds.), *Handbook of bereavement research: Consequences, coping, and care* (pp. 647–669). Washington, DC: American Psychological Association.

Follette, V. M., Ruzek, J. I., & Abueg, F. R. (1998). A contextual analysis of trauma: Theoretical considerations. In V. M. Follette, J. I. Ruzek, & F. R. Abueg (Eds.), *Cognitive behavioral therapies for trauma* (pp. 3–14). New York: Guilford Press.

Goodman, R. F. (2002a). *Caring for kids after trauma and death: A guide for parents and professionals.* Downloaded at www.aboutourkids com/crisis_guide02.pdf. New York: New York University Child Study Center.

Goodman, R. F. (2002b). *Talking to kids about their art.* New York University Child Study Center, New York, at http://www.aboutourkids.org/articles/talking tokidsabouttheirart.html

Jacobs, S. (1999). *Traumatic grief: Diagnosis, treatment, and prevention.* Philadelphia, PA: Brunner/Mazel.

Koh, C. V. (2000). *How children grieve.* Unpublished training notes from the Jewish Board of Family and Children's Services Loss and Bereavement Program. New York: JBFCS.

Layne, C., Saltzman, W., & Pynoos, R. (2002). *Trauma/grief-focused groups psychotherapy program manual.* Los Angeles: UCLA Psychiatry Service.

Noppe, L. D. & Noppe, I. C. (1996). Ambiguity in adolescent understandings of death. In C. A. Corr & D. E. Balk (Eds.), *Handbook of adolescent death and bereavement* (pp. 25–41). New York: Springer Publishing Company.

O'Donohue, W., Fanetti, M., & Elliott, A. (1998). Trauma in children. In V. M. Follette, J. I. Ruzek, & F. R. Abueg (Eds.), *Cognitive behavioral therapies for trauma* (pp. 355–382). New York: Guilford Press.

Pilaro, L. (2002). *Development of affective competence.* Unpublished conceptual model from the Jewish Board of Family and Children's Services Loss and Bereavement Program. New York: JBFCS.

Piper, W. E., McCallum, M., & Azim, H. F. A. (1992). *Adaptation to loss through short term group psychotherapy.* New York: Guilford Press.

Prigerson, H. G. & Jacobs, S. C. (2002). Traumatic grief as a distinct disorder: A rationale, consensus criteria and a preliminary empirical test. In M. S. Stroebe, R. O., Hannsson, W. Stroebe, & H. Schut (Eds.), *Handbook of bereavement research: Consequences, coping, and care* (pp. 613–645). Washington, DC: American Psychological Association.

Russell, P. (1998). *Trauma, repetition and affect regulation: The work of Paul Russell,* [J. Teicholz. EDD (Ed.)]. New York: The Other Press.

Saltzman, W. R., Pynoos, R. S., Steinberg, A. M., Aisenberg, E., & Layne, C. M. (2001). Trauma-and grief-focused intervention for adolescents exposed to community violence: Results of a school-based screening and group treatment protocol. *Group Dynamics: Theory, Research, and Practice, 5*(4), 291–303.

Schilling, R. F., Koh, N., Abramovitz, R., & Gilbert, L. (1992). Bereavement groups for inner-city children. *Research on Social Work Practice, 2*(3), 405–419.

Schoeman, L. & Kreitzman, R. (1997). Death of a parent: Group intervention with bereaved children and their caregivers. *Psychoanalysis and Psychotherapy, 14*(2), 221–245.

Spring, D. (1994). Art therapy as a visual dialogue. In M. B. Williams & J. F. Sommer (Eds.), *Handbook of posttraumatic therapy* (pp. 337–351). Westport, CT: Greenwood Press.

Stubenbort, K., Donnnelly, G. R., & Cohen, J. A. (2001). Cognitive-behavioral group therapy for bereaved adults and children following an air disaster. *Group Dynamics: Theory, Research, and Practice, 5*(4), 261–276.

Trad, P. V. & Greenblatt, E. (1990). Psychological aspects of child distress: Development and the spectrum of coping responses. In L. E. Arnold (Ed)., *Childhood stress* (pp. 23–49). New York: John Wiley and Sons, Inc.

van der Kolk, B. A. (1996). The black hole of trauma. In B. A. van der Kolk, A. C. McFarlane, & L. Weisaeth (Eds.), *Traumatic stress: The effects of overwhelming experience on mind, body, and society* (pp. 182–213). New York: Guilford Press.

Webb, N. B. (1993). Counseling and therapy for the bereaved child. In N. B. Webb (Ed.), *Helping bereaved children: A handbook for practitioners* (pp. 43–58). New York: Guilford Press.

Worden, J. W. (1991). *Grief counseling and grief therapy: A handbook for the mental health practitioner* (2nd ed.). New York: Springer Publishing Company.

Worden, J. W. (1996). *Children and grief: When a parent dies.* New York: Guilford Press.

Appendix A

Bibliography for Children and Adolescents who are Dealing with Loss

For Parents

Grollman, Earl. (1976). *Talking about death: A dialogue between parent and child.* Boston: Beacon Press.

Jackson, E. N. (1966). *Telling a child about death.* Des Moines, IA: Meredith Press.

For Primary School Children

Buscaglia, Leo. (1983). *Fall of Freddie the Leaf.* New York: G. P. Putnam & Sons.

DePaola, Tomie. (1997). *Nana upstairs and Nana downstairs.* New York: G. Putnam & Sons.

Fassler, Joan. (1982). *My Grandpa died today.* New York: Human Resources Press, Inc.

Miles, Miska. (1971). *Annie the Old One.* Boston: Little, Brown & Company.

Sheppard, Carol H. (1998). *Brave Bart: A story for traumatized and grieving children.* Grosse Point Woods, MI: Institute for Trauma and Loss in Children.

For Middle Grade Children or Older

Blume, Judy. (1981). *Tiger eyes.* New York: Dell Publishing Company.

Frank, Anne. (1963). *The diary of a young girl.* New York: Washington Square Press.

Smith, Doris B. (1973). *A taste of blackberries.* New York: Thomas Cromwell.

White, E. B. (1952). *Charlotte's web.* New York: Harper & Row, Inc.

For Teens

Kemetz, Jill. (1981). *How it feels when a parent dies.* New York: Alfred Knopf, Inc.

Le Shan, Eda. (1979). *Learning to say goodbye (when a parent dies).* New York: Macmillan Press.

Appendix B

Annotated Multimedia Suggestions for Confronting Traumatic Grief

Movies and Television

Thomas, Chris (Producer). (1994). *The lion king* [Motion Picture]. United States: Walt Disney Pictures Disney Productions.

The evil Uncle Scar tells Simba all the reasons that Simba caused Musafa's (his father's) death. At the end, Nala helps Simba understand that Musafa's death was not his fault and that the father always is with him in memory.

Spielberg, Steven (Director). (1982). *E.T.: the extra-terrestrial* [Motion Picture]. United States: Universal Studios.

This movie may be a significant film for young people. It is fantasy vs. reality of death since ET comes back to life. It details the moving pain and struggle of accepting a death. The film ends with ET being remembered at home in the sky . . . metaphorical for the person being in heaven?

Home Box Office (Producer). *Def poetry.* An HBO Series.

Young poets perform some of their work. Some of these works could be easily represent current hip-hop music. Most poems performed have significant implications for how youth may view the world.

Contemporary Songs

Black Eyed Peas. (2003). Anxiety. On *Elephunt* [CD]. (Track 12). New York: A&M.
Black Eyed Peas. (2003). Where is the love. On *Elephunt* [CD]. (Track 13). New York: A&M.
Creed. (2001). *Weathered* [CD]. New York: Wind-up.
Listings of lyrics and albums can be found at www.creed.com. This album has several songs with poignant messages.
Whose got my back now. (Track 4); Weathered. (Track 8)
One last breath. (Track 5); Signs. (Track 3)

Lavigne, Avril. (2002). *Let Go* [CD]. New York: Arista.
Complicated. (Track 2); Unwanted. (Track 6)

Linkin Park. (2002). In the end. On *Hybrid theory* [CD]. (Track 8). New York: Warner Bros.

Pink. (2001). Don't let me get me. On *Mizundastood* [CD]. (Track 2). New York: Arista.

Simon, Carly. (1994). Like a River. On *Letters Never Sent* [CD]. (Track 4). New York: Arista.

This song may be excellent for the caregivers and highlights fights over the deceased's belongings.

12 Group Work with Adolescent Sexual Offenders in Community-based Treatment

Christy Driscoll and Keith T. Fadelici

Introduction

The most popular modality currently in use within specialized adolescent sexual offender treatment is group work. In our practice with low to medium risk adolescent sexual offenders in an outpatient treatment program set at Astor Counseling Services in Poughkeepsie, New York, we too use group as the principal modality in our multi-modality approach. While we inherited from our predecessor this preference for a group approach to the sex-offender-specific, cognitive behavioral therapy, we have developed our own rationale for the primacy of group in our practice. That rationale has shaped and informed every aspect of our assessment and treatment process and it is the purpose of this chapter to describe that rationale. Our hope is that we may provoke further reflection on why we, as clinicians, are currently practicing in the ways that many of us are and that this chapter may stimulate research to further substantiate the speculations and claims made here.

We begin with a brief discussion of the etiology of adolescent sexual offending behaviors as described in the current literature and as experienced within our own practice. Secondly, we provide an overview of the group treatment process using David Finklehor's four preconditions to sexual offending as described in *Pathways* (1996) by Timothy Kahn. Finally we look at the question of why a group treatment approach might be a preferable modality in which to treat adolescents who have sexually offended.

Description of the Population

To date there are no typologies that can predict the likelihood of a teenager sexually acting out. However, there is a need to be able to identify and characterize this population and the literature points to certain variables.

Among adolescent sexual offenders males predominate in both the literature and the population served at the Astor Counseling Services. Although the number of female referrals continues to climb the majority or 96% of the caseload is male.

The field has struggled to understand the correlation of victimization (specifically) and trauma (generally) with sexually abusive behavior.

Throughout the literature there is a positive correlation between the adolescent sexual offenders suffering from their own sexual victimization as well as physical abuse. Although the statistics vary widely from 20 to 80% (Burton, 2001; Ryan, 1999; Ryan, Miyoshi, Metzner, Krugman, & Fryer, 1996) for sexual abuse depending on the nature of the population being studied and 40 to 80% for physical abuse there remains the positive correlation throughout. This traumagenic approach to looking at the etiology of sexual offense is similar to social learning theory: what is done to us we do to others. Biological research also indicates that there is significant brain and chemical changes that occur to severely and persistently abused children resulting in depression, anxiety, hyper or hypo responsiveness, withdrawal, aggression, etc. (Burton, 2001). Trauma work is being done by 82–89% of the adolescent sexual offender programs in this country and there are many that believe this is the core issue (Burton, 2001). Of the adolescents we serve 41% are positive for a sexual and/or physical abuse history. Similarly exposure to pornographic material and early sexual stimulation is correlated to sexually acting out. Burton suggests that 80–85% of adolescent sexual offenders have been exposed to pornography and a smaller number exposed to hard core child porn (Burton, 2001). There also may be a danger in overestimating the significance of a trauma history. Most often victims of sexual abuse do not sexually victimize others. In many cases such as the population we serve (low-medium risk adolescent offenders,) the statistics indicate past sexual victimization is not a primary factor and in other cases is not an issue at all.

Social relatedness and the appearance of strong interpersonal bonds also seem to be lacking. The ability to pick up social cues or respond empathically to people is difficult for many. We see in the literature and most frequently in our own group experience that youthful sexual offenders have significant deficits in peer relationships. They are either inept at simple conversational skills, or their self-esteem is so diminished that their ability to approach opposite or same sex interests are compromised. Very often these children are aggressive or considered bullies and are alienated. Not only is social isolation and poor relatedness a strong component in the development of offending behavior, research has shown that social ineptitude, social isolation, and a lack of good supports and close emotional relationships are all related to the presence of disturbed functioning and to post-treatment relapse (Marshall, 1989).

Similarly prevalent in this population are academic dysfunction and learning disabilities. The Center for Sex Offender Management in a document issued in 2000 stated that 30–60% of juvenile sex offenders exhibit learning disabilities and academic dysfunction. Although other research has not so specifically identified poor academic performance as an issue they have indicated that large percentages (60%) were known to have truancy, learning disabilities, and/or behavior problems at school (Ryan, Miyoshi, Metzner, Krugman, & Fryer, 1996). Often times receptive and expressive language is impaired, limiting effective communication with their peer group. In our clinic

44% of the adolescents suffer with some form of academic dysfunction or learning disability and more often than not their school experience is fraught with failure and frustration. Due to their frustration and poor self-esteem in the classroom they often begin to divert attention away from academics by becoming disruptive. This further alienates them from their peer group, makes them a target for punishment from teachers, and tends to build for them a reputation as unruly and uncooperative teenagers.

There is significant evidence to suggest that dysfunctional familial and parent–child relationships can greatly contribute to offense behavior. In a study cited by Burton, Nesmith, and Badten (1997) Waggoner and Boyd concluded that etiology of sexually abusive behavior could be traced to ineffective parenting, poor relationships between children and parents, lack of community supports, and to the youths' disposition. A report issued by the Office of Juvenile Justice and Delinquency Prevention in 2001 cited many different research projects that indicate many juvenile offenders have experienced physical and/or emotional separations from one or both of their parents, negative, aggressive, and interruptive styles of communication are more prevalent, and poor or inadequate supervision was cited.

Coinciding, in some cases, with family dysfunction is the presence of increased psychiatric diagnosis and substance abuse. In their review of the professional literature Righthand and Welch (2001) reported that Miner, Siekert, and Ackland found that 60% of biological fathers had some substance abuse history, 28% had criminal histories, and although mothers were less likely to have these issues they still ranked at 28% for substance abuse and 17% with criminal histories. Mothers were more likely than fathers to have psychiatric treatment (23% versus 13%) (2001). Coinciding with parental psychiatric diagnosis and treatment the literature suggests that adolescent sexual offenders have a diagnosable psychiatric disorder in 80% of the cases. Commonly diagnosed disorders include conduct disorder, impulse control disorder, and schizoid, avoidant, as well as higher rates of depression or depressive symptoms.

Not so clearly defined in the literature is the role of substance abuse in sexually offending behavior. It would seem natural to assume that decreased inhibition, along with impaired judgment and impulse control resulting from substance and alcohol abuse would correlate to a higher incidence of sexual offense, but the literature does not currently demonstrate a direct relationship between substance/alcohol abuse and the crime. However, because of its disinhibiting potential it needs to be looked at in initial assessment as well as in on-going treatment. Statistically at the clinic we identified that 33% of our adolescents had problematic substance abuse either themselves or in their home environment.

Each of these identifying factors has a potentially negative impact on the ability to relate to others. Connection or relationship to others provides the individual with essential ingredients for growth and development. When a child's ability to absorb that nurturance from others is hampered they will be more likely to strike out in an aggressive manner. The following is an overview of how these deficits are addressed in treatment.

Group Treatment Process

The four preconditions of sexual offending form the backbone of the therapeutic process we employ. They succinctly identify four factors universally evident in sexual offending and in so doing identify four points at which sexual offending behavior can be avoided and/or prevented.

The four preconditions are:

1.   Having motivation to offend;
2.   Overcoming internal barriers to offending;
3.   Overcoming external barriers to offending; and
4.   Overcoming victim resistance. (Kahn, 1996)

If any one of these preconditions is absent the offense will not occur and therefore the work of treatment and, more specifically, the work of the adolescent offender is to decrease their motivation to offend, increase the strength of their internal and external barriers, and to increase their awareness and sensitivity to victim resistance.

Reduction of motivation begins with the identification of one's own motivations for the original offense. The most commonly identified motivational factors in our groups include: need for affection and/or attention, anger at parent figures, anger at the victim, exposure to pornography or erotica, and reactive response to adolescent's own victimization (sexual or non-sexual abuse or neglect.)

Many offenders will initially identify their motivation as sexual arousal or even sexual curiosity; however, these factors are most often not central to their later understandings of their motivation for offending. When details of the offense and the other pressures, issues, and influences at play in the adolescents life around the time of the offense are carefully detailed they often indicate significant emotional needs that appear to feed into or fuel the sexual impulses. Some group members appear to take comfort in their original sexual-arousal or "I was horny" explanation for offending. Perhaps it serves as a source of a distorted masculine pride. Resistance to considering other motivational factors is sometimes combated by pointing out that the inability to control one's sexual-arousal response (as would be the case in many higher-risk adolescent offenders) is a condition that is far more difficult to address and successfully treat.

While some clients cling to the "sexual arousal" component of their motivation other clients have eschewed this component completely. These clients tend to view themselves as victims of parental neglect or abuse who offended against others as either a cry for help or as a cumulative explosion of pent-up anger and hurt. This asexual-motivation-theory is often rebutted by asking the client why he didn't punch someone, steal, or set a fire. The specifics of the offense, including the details of the sexuality contained in the aggression, must be carefully explored and incorporated into the client's understanding of their own motivational factors.

The question of motivation is not resolved in a single session or group module. It is an issue that is visited and revisited, serving as a leitmotif throughout treatment. With each account of their offense the question of motivation is discussed. In one exercise the individual member's account of the offense is addressed by the group and explored for the purpose of increasing the detail of the story, a process that has often helped to clarify the member's motivation. This is especially helpful when the offense-account is seen firmly set within the context of other factors and events in the member's life. Members have moved from believing that their offense was about "sexual arousal" to seeing how it might have been more strongly linked to the fact that they were in their third foster care home at the time, or their parents had consistently failed to show affection or love to them.

Every motivation for offending is a need. The offense is a failed, destructive, unacceptable attempt to meet a perfectly valid need. The treatment process is an attempt not only to avoid these destructive behaviors but also to train the offender to meet their needs in an appropriate, life-affirming, effective manner. We believe that this approach is not only consistent with our professional ethics and personal values but is also the most effective means to avoiding further perpetration.

Internal barriers are constituted by: caring about others, knowledge about right and wrong, and fear of getting caught (Kahn, 1996). We discuss these internal barriers as the functions of the person's conscience. It is our internal barriers that stop the vast majority of human beings from offensive behaviors of all kinds. How many of us are not motivated to strike out and take what we feel we need and/or deserve but has been denied us? For most people adequate motivation to perform crimes exists on a fairly regular basis. However, most people in most situations where the motivation exists still do not perform the crime and while there are still two other barriers after this one we believe that internal barriers or a sense of conscience is what stops most people from offending.

The work on internal barriers functions on two levels: 1. Psycho-educational Function, and 2. Nurturing and Practice of Conscience. These two levels of the work are not in practice divisible, although they are usually distinguishable. Conscience, values, morality, and ethics are subjects that can be taught and learned. Attaining knowledge in regards to these makes one more capable of actually practicing the concepts.

Educating young people regarding conscience is in large measure about raising awareness of their own existing but unidentified sense of right and wrong. For the most part the adolescent offenders are not lacking in morality or ethical knowledge but their sense of right and wrong is often inarticulate. An inarticulate idea or value has no word attached to it and therefore cannot be referenced or easily drawn into consciousness when the situation demands its application or consideration. The inarticulate morality is a "gut feeling" of right and wrong. But gut feelings lack nuance and cannot be applied to the subtleties of most real-life moral dilemmas. The inarticulate morality either stops one from committing an act or it does not; there can be no practice of an ethical process of reflection or consideration based upon a gut feeling and, therefore, a gut feeling does not allow for responsibility.

Creating a language that fits a young person's morality and value system increases the offender's awareness of issues of right and wrong and provides the tools by which they can make ethical choices in a particular situation. However, abstract thinking is often not a strength of many of our clients. Therefore attempts at ethical dialogues about what makes something wrong or right often become one-sided and the clients are unable to demonstrate an understanding of the material.

Recently we employed a new process to engage the young men in one of our groups on these topics. We started by asking the group to brainstorm a list of heroes. Once that list was generated the members described why the individuals on the list could be seen as heroic, thus creating a second list, a list of characteristics that the members could recognize as valuable. We then generated a list of anti-values, eventually introducing the idea of these values and anti-values being on a continuum. The members seemed to find it relatively easy after this process to identify and discuss the values that were lacking or were weak in themselves at the time of the offense. Once all the members identified the weaknesses of their internal barrier at the time of the offense we gave them the assignment of identifying how they would teach a student to "respect others" (an oft chosen value) if they had all the resources in the world available to them. Out of this hypothetical the members identified ways they could increase the strength of values that played a role in their offense.

The third precondition of sexual offending is the overcoming of any external barriers (Kahn, 1996). External barriers are obstacles to the opportunity to offend. To have the opportunity to offend one must either create or be given access to a potential victim and the time and place to perpetrate the crime. If a person has the motivation to commit a crime and lacks the strength of conscience to stop himself it is essential that they not be afforded the opportunity to offend.

In multi-modality treatment the individual client as well as those on a supportive team are trained to be aware of opportunities to offend and to intervene to eliminate or limit such an opportunity. Parents and the offending child are informed at the point of intake that the opportunity for offending is to be both avoided and prohibited. A safety-plan is developed with the client and the parents. The safety-plan includes round-the-clock supervision whenever other children or vulnerable persons are in the presence of the client. Opportunities for offending such as babysitting jobs or any other situation that would place the client in a position of authority over other children are prohibited. A preliminary set of high-risk situations are identified early in treatment usually consisting of the persons, places, and situations related directly to their original offense. The client contracts with the parents, the probation officer, and the clinicians that he will avoid high-risk situations and report them. Clients agree that if they find themselves alone in a room with younger children and no adult present they are to leave that room. If asked to babysit they are expected to decline. If substance abuse or alcohol use were factors in the original offense these too are viewed as high-risk situations.

External barriers are generally outside of the individual and are imposed upon the person by external forces. Therefore the strengthening of the external barriers in the life of an adolescent is work that largely falls to the parents, the family, and the community. In our monthly parent group we work to heighten the awareness of parents and family members as to what constitutes adequate supervision as well as what are appropriate and inappropriate materials, experiences, and responsibilities for an adolescent.

While exposure to pornography was listed above as a motivational factor we raise it here because of its relationship to parent and community failure to protect the client from unnecessary exposure to pornographic material. The client often comes to describe such exposure as a fairly immediate and direct trigger to the actual offense. Some parents believed that the pornography they hid in their bedroom was safe and that the children were not aware of its existence. Others argue that some exposure to pornography is normal and healthy behavior. In response we attempt to increase the parents' understanding of the impact of explicit sexual material on young children and explain that the resulting stimulation can be overwhelming, confusing, and damaging, not to mention criminal. These young people have not developed the ability to control or manage high levels of sexual stimulation, as the clients demonstrated by offending.

We also introduce the notion that pornography itself, whether in the hands of an adult or child, is problematic in as much as it objectifies persons and undermines or weakens the connection between sexuality and *personhood*. That loss of sensitivity to the *personhood* of the other, their intrinsic value, is at the core of every sexual and non-sexual offensive act. The cultural acceptance of objectification of others, for the purpose of personal stimulation or as a sales ploy in the marketplace, is a meta-narrative in all of our lives and we believe our clients and their families will benefit from an increased consciousness of its impact on others and on themselves.

The final barrier to offending is the resistance of the victim (Kahn, 1996). Unlike motivation and conscience the victim's resistance is not the property of the offender and that, in itself, is an important concept for the offender to grasp. Even the external barriers are focused on the offender in so far as they are about restraining him from taking certain action or having the opportunity to perform certain acts. There is in effect nothing the offender or the family can do to increase victim resistance to insure that it stops them from offending if all else fails.

However, the client can learn to recognize various forms of resistance and may even be aided in developing greater desire not to violate another's autonomy. The clients are educated about the impact of sexual assault on victims, discuss at great length the emotional scarring and developmental impact of such an assault on a young person, and write and re-write letters (not sent), to their victims acknowledging their offense and apologizing for the harm they caused. This is all done in the hope that with understanding of the damage sexual perpetration inflicts upon a victim the offender might, when confronted with victim resistance, stop themselves from carrying through an assault.

Victim resistance takes many forms but the three principal forms of resistance are physical resistance, verbal resistance, and fleeing. Physical resistance is easily understood and difficult, though not impossible, for the offender to misconstrue. The most common offender explanation for misinterpreting physical resistance is: "we were playing around—I didn't think she was serious." Verbal resistance, or when the victim says "no," is overcome by an offender by failing to hear the message and reporting: "I didn't hear her say no and if I did I would have stopped." Others will also explain that they didn't think she meant it. Fleeing is any kind of fearful response to the assault. This may take the form of trying to run away, calling for help, telling an adult, crying, or being upset. When a victim is a young child it is the flee response that most often concerns the adolescent offender. The child is therefore often groomed, or made to feel comfortable with the behavior over a period of time. The offender's consciousness is raised through treatment about the various forms of resistance and to their own methods of overcoming or circumventing those barriers. The offender's explanations for how or why they did not appropriately respond to that resistance are dissected, challenged, and discussed.

Some adolescent offenders have little or no understanding of the significance of age and the relevance it plays in a child's ability to consent to a sexual act. Developmental, moral, and legal distinctions are explained, discussed, and taught.

However, recognizing one's own grooming behaviors and the victim's various forms of resistance will not in itself stop the offender from offending. Some clients argue early in treatment that they don't need to continue in the program because: "when I offended I didn't think it was a big deal. Now I know it does real and potentially life-long harm to a victim so I'll never do it again." One of our favorite responses to this argument is: "You're right, offending does hurt a victim. But so what? What difference does that make?" This question is intended to generate thinking about the distinction between knowing something and caring about something, leading to further conversation about caring about something enough to sacrifice a desire for it. Without a willingness to feel discomfort in order to benefit or, at the very least, prevent harming another, there is little value to identifying the "right" and "wrong" things to do.

This quality is identified as *empathy*. To foster empathy in the members of the client group we request that each member identify a moment from their week in which they experienced empathy for another. The members identify others in their family, school, or neighborhood who have suffered and publicly acknowledge feeling sorrow for that person or being happy for that person when they have had an accomplishment. The exercise is a practice in caring for others.

Beyond these four barriers or preconditions to offending the client identifies their high-risk situations and appropriate strategies to manage those situations in order to reduce the risk of a re-offense. That listing of high-risk situations with their corresponding behavioral strategies is called the Relapse Prevention Plan (Kahn, 1996). This plan is developed by the client with input from the therapist, the other group members, the probation officer, and their family members. The clients are also expected to demonstrate that the strategies identified can actually work for them by reporting each week about high-risk situations and how they managed those situations using a strategy. The Relapse Prevention Plan is an extension of the initial safety plan and one that extends beyond the limits of treatment and into the remainder of the client's life.

Why Group?

Group therapy is the most common format of treatment with sexual abusers. Advantages to group work listed in *Practice Standards and Guidelines for Members of the Association for the Treatment of Sexual Abusers* (ATSA, 2001) include: Group treatment is more economical than individual therapy; clients are often more accepting of feedback from more advanced clients; seeing the progress of other members offers hope for positive change; clients may reveal a greater range of thoughts, feelings, and behavior when interacting with other members; and group interactions provide an opportunity to evaluate and target social and relationship skills.

The majority of these advantages of group work noted by ATSA are referring to the fruits of what the Association for the Advancement of Social Work with Groups calls the "democratic process" (1999, p. 2) that characterizes group work. The worker-to-group and worker-to-member relationship "characterized by egalitarianism and reciprocity" (1999, p. 2) aids in the creation of a therapeutic environment that allows for member-to-member assistance, self-help, and healthy human interaction within a group therapy process.

There is often a palpable relief for new members upon arriving in the group after a six-week, individual assessment process. This relief seems to be due to several factors: the client discovers, after much anticipation, that his fellow group members are actually his peers, and not a group of drooling, perverted monsters; the client has concrete proof that it is possible to move through "the work" and that healing, learning, and graduation are real, achievable goals as evidenced by the senior members of the group. Perhaps most significantly, they see that they are not alone in making such a grievous error in judgment, nor in struggling with the forces and drives that played a part in their offending. The group becomes a place where they learn it is possible to take full responsibility for an awful offense against others without having to completely sever oneself from the human family. Kindness and friendliness are not inconsistent with owning one's offense. In fact, these positive human interactions are the very sustenance that, in many cases, reduces the motivation to behave in offensive ways.

The lack of effective social interaction, relatedness, communication, and bonding are common deficits in sexual offenders (Hudson & Ward, 2000). These deficits are addressed by work in the group setting. The members are expected to interact with each other in appropriate ways. When a member checks-in that a relative has died or they have suffered a loss the other members are challenged to respond in an appropriate and direct manner. Often such interactions and common courtesies are quite foreign to the members. In our community-based setting each member is expected to say goodbye at the end of a session with a handshake and direct eye contact. Such contact, physical and emotional, is an opportunity for members to develop greater levels of comfort in the presence of others and to practice appropriate and respectful ways of interacting.

In many forms of psychotherapy a safehouse condition is established within the context of the therapeutic relationship (Fox, 1993). A safehouse provides a retreat for the purpose of healing and renewal. With retreat come perspective and the calm and confidence needed to act and/or change. A safehouse is an apt analogy for the therapeutic process and applies in varying degrees to all modalities.

Eda Goldstein (1995) succinctly states: "The client–worker relationship exists for a purpose. It focuses on the client's need" (p. 201). In her discussion of ego-oriented therapists' use of self in treatment Goldstein describes realistic and unrealistic components of the client–therapist relationship (1995). This tension between the "real relationship" and the "unrealistic relationship" is a well-established helping-tool throughout most psychotherapies. In thinking about our work with sexual-offending adolescents we might reframe this distinction as the meeting of Otherness and the meeting of Self. Otherness, in this sense, would represent a "real relationship" experience and a meeting of Self would represent the "unrealistic relationship" or transference. The offending clients usually need work in both of these arenas.

With histories of physical abuse, sexual abuse, learning disabilities, and trauma-related symptoms these clients are clearly bearing the scars of environmental and familial dysfunction. A safehouse approach in which they receive nurturing, supportive and warm acceptance and direction is obviously advisable.

However, they are also perpetrators of offenses against others, usually significantly weaker, younger, and smaller than themselves. Sexually abusive adolescents also tend to be poorly related, impulsive, and aggressive. Cognitive-behavioral approaches to adolescent treatment, as described in the prior section, have been strongly supported in the field, although not well researched. The strength of that approach is in its focus on educating and training the clients to recognize abusive behavioral patterns and to develop the skills needed to alter those behavioral patterns.

The most popular modality currently in use for this cognitive-behavioral therapy is group work. We too use group as the principal modality with family, individual, and parent group as the other modalities in our multimodality approach. There is little or no literature found to support by outcome studies the primacy of group with this population.

However, in our conceptualization of sexual offending behavior as a difficulty, primarily, in one's relationship to Otherness we find a compelling argument in favor of the group preference. In individual work Otherness is contained in a single therapeutic, professional figure focused on the needs of the client themselves. The individual session is exclusively focused on the Self. Even a significant portion of the relationship of the client to the therapist is commonly understood and interpreted to be further manifestations of the client's Self projected upon the screen of the therapist.

In family sessions there is an opportunity for a greater experience of Otherness but one that is significantly weakened by the fact that many of these children are poorly individuated from other family members. The family members, especially parental figures, may tend to be experienced as extensions of Self. In other instances the offending child, identified as "the problem," will become the sole focus of family work allowing the Self-project to once again take precedence.

It is in the group context, we believe, that the experience of Otherness is maximized allowing for the client's relationship to Otherness to come into focus. In group there are multiple faces, multiple screens, and so attempts to exclusively focus on the Self tend to meet with frustration. The other members ultimately demand attention; unlike with the therapist, whose sole purpose is the client.

This is not to suggest that the function of group therapy is system-focused. The function of the group work being done in sex-offender-specific treatment is to focus on the individual characteristics of the adolescent offender that have encouraged or fueled the abusive behavior patterns. Family sessions primarily focus on the familial, environmental, interpersonal factors contributing to the abusive behaviors and on the family-based strengths by which the behavior may be altered.

While the group work focuses on each individual offender's personal characteristics, strengths, and deficits, the milieu of group provides a social context, larger than that of family, for a treatment process aimed at impacting an essentially interpersonal issue.

Conclusion

The four preconditions of sexual abuse provide a guide for examining and developing a detailed understanding of the offensive behavior as well as the conditions that led to it. That process helps us to identify key areas or high-risk categories around which the client and the family's work needs to be centered. In the end, all offensive behavior is a weakness or failure in our relatedness to others, to ourselves, and to the world. Group places the healing process into the very context of that brokenness: one's relationship to Otherness.

References

Association for the Advancement of Social Work with Groups, Inc. (1999). *Standards for social work practice with groups.* Cleveland, OH: AASWG, Inc.

ATSA Professional Issues Committee. (2001). *Practice standards and guidelines for members of the Association for the Treatment of Sexual Abusers.* Beaverton, OR: Association for the Treatment of Sexual Abusers.

Burton, D. L. (2001). *Adolescent sexual abusers: A basic primer.* Ann Arbor, MI: David L. Burton.

Burton, D.L., Nesmith, A.A., & Badten, L. (1997). Clinician's views on sexually aggressive children and their families: A theoretical exploration. *Child Abuse and Neglect, 21,* 157–170.

Center for Sex Offender Management. (2000). *Myths and facts about sex offenders.* Washington DC: U.S. Department of Justice.

Fox, R. (1993). *Elements of the helping process: A guide for clinicians.* New York: The Haworth Press.

Goldstein, E. (1995). *Ego psychology and social work practice.* New York: The Free Press.

Hudson, S. & Ward, T. (2000). Interpersonal competency in sex offenders. *Behavior Modification, 24,* 494–527.

Kahn, T. J. (1996). *Pathways: A guided workbook for youth beginning treatment* (Revised ed.). Brandon, VT: Safer Society Press.

Marshall, W. L. (1989). Intimacy, loneliness and sexual offenders. *Behavioral Research Therapy, 27,* 491–503.

Righthand, S. & Welch, C. (2001) *Juveniles who have sexually offended, A review of the professional literature report.* Washington, DC: U.S. Department of Justice, Office of Juvenile Justice and Delinquency Prevention.

Ryan, G. (1999). Treatment of sexually abusive youth: The evolving consensus. *Journal of Interpersonal Violence, 14,* 422–436.

Ryan, G., Miyoshi, T. J., Metzner, J. L., Krugman, R. D.,& Fryer, G. (1996). Trends in a national sample of sexually abusive youths. *Journal of the American Academy of Child Psychiatry, 35,* 17–25.

Index